SUPERNATURAL PHENOMENA
IN THE BIBLE EXPLAINED

By: Denise Freed

GOD AND SCIENCE ARE NOT AT ODDS
WITH EACH OTHER

BY: Denise Freed

ISBN: 9780989881319

USA

TABLE OF CONTENTS

INTRODUCTION

The Israelite lineage was born out of love for family and for God through many generations; a God Whom was little understood until Abraham, a man of great faith and love in sacrifice, was able to command on this planet the knowledge that catapulted an empire of Israelite into the world and around the globe.

It was this heart-felt love, manifested through Abraham's and Sarah's lineage through their son, Isaac, and later their grandson, Jacob, who was renamed Israel. Jacob/Israel's twelve sons would continue in God's blessings and would earn the right to understand the God of Heaven. This was accomplished by tests which were applied to these people by God. Through these tests and lessons given to them, they learned obedience to God over time. Each generation had to be tested. Some of them passed the tests to remain true to God while others failed these tests and were punished by being turned over to the dark forces that had misguided them. Each generation, for each lineage of Abraham and Sarah had to be built upon struggles, and minor and sometimes major infractions in their trouble, while they discovered why love for family and the world was so necessary for them to grow. Their strength came only after great struggles and great loss sometimes. It was in their struggle that they understood what was to be won in their doing right as God had taught them.

By their efforts in trying to serve God and keep His commandments, Israel became the example to the world that the God of Abraham and Jacob/Israel, the God who created all things, could be trusted as the only true guidance for mankind. Abraham's struggle will not be in vain, his faith which rested in the God of Heaven continues to spread to all the families of the earth, as each person learns the lesson of faith taught to Abraham and his chosen lineage through Jacob/Israel.

The struggles were only part of the story. Each child who had to learn the right path was to be taught by God through the angel messengers He would send to each one of them. The story of the Bible was built upon the spiritual gifts God brought to each child who sought Him. The spiritual messages given to the Israelite comprise the majority of the messages from God in the Old and New Testaments, through spiritistic methods, we could call psychic or mediumistic talents today. It was in this secondary struggle to reach upward to God and to practice the arts of divination, that they were able to reach God in the several means of messages they received, and many of which are recorded in the scriptures.

This book is meant to reintroduce the Bible in the original form of spiritual beliefs so that you, the reader, might see this ancient book with a renewed love for God's word, meant to lighten the load in life, and not to create a burden of unreasonable rules to follow aimlessly, which Bible revisionists added and altered in the Holy Scriptures over the centuries. Christ complained about those same rule-making religious leaders in His day as hypocrites. Today, these false teachers share their rules for money making and harsh punishments sent by God as the path to Heaven, while their followers learn nothing of the true path of character refinement, taught by the angels of Heaven to mankind.

As regards the most important questions of religion, the various churches hold conflicting views. Man, being fallible, is at best a dubious guide in these matters. To reach the truth of Heaven there can be only one way, the good spirits who live in that place must provide it, and teach mankind directly, without human intermediaries clouding up the message with their own interpretations of the messages from Heaven, it is the only way. If there is a beyond populated by a world of spirits, then conclusive proof can only be had if those spirits will visit and enlighten us, for they alone are able to tell us the truth about the great questions relating to an after-life. So long as this gap between the good spirit world and our own remains unbridged, mankind will remain in the darkness of uncertainty and will continue to live in doubt of a God of wisdom.

Today, people laugh at those who speak of the bare possibility of establishing communication between the world of men and that of spirits. Those who have no understanding of a subject often ridicule it, especially if it conflicts with their own beliefs. Rather than try to understand, some people with the loudest voices speak against the unknown and condemn it so that others would also reject new ideas, and keep tradition controlling their future rather than truth. It is tradition that is the greatest enemy of truth. Tradition is often followed by each generation without being questioned at all, even if it makes no sense to the followers. And so it has always been the same pattern regarding any revelation or invention. In hopes to enlighten you, I offer the Bible as it was meant to be read, as a spiritual guidance, taught by the spirits who live in Heaven.

5

OUR NATURAL ABILITY

Since the beginning of the time that humans have been on this planet, they have been able to communicate with the world of spirits. Science doesn't always agree with this, but then scientists are only learning of natural forces through experimentation, observation or just like the rest of society, and they don't yet know the rules of creation themselves. We have many instances of spiritual communication from the Bible stories and also from people's experiences.

We live in a world in the visible material habitat as well as the mostly invisible, but influential, spirit world. There is constant interaction between the two daily in every person's life. Most are not even aware of it because they are so used to it. It is said that up to fifty percent of a person's thoughts can be influenced by the invisible forces around them. After all, God created us as spirits with an ethereal body first, and now we are incarnated (which means in the flesh) in a condensed form, we call a material body. So in the clearest explanation of our state of existence, we are spirits living in a shell of material flesh. We live in two worlds. Most people are so caught up in daily activities of gathering and accomplishing for the material existence portion, that they happily ignore the impending return to the spirit state only a few years ahead.

When our physical body dies, it returns to the earth, while our spirit enters the world of spirits and continues to live forever. The Old Testament says,"All go to the same place; all come from dust, and to dust all return" (Eccl 3:20). People who are clairvoyant can see into the spirit world and those who are clairaudient can hear the spirits. In the Old Testament, a person who was clairvoyant or had other spiritually sensitive methods of discerning the spirit world, were called seers, prophets or priests, whether male or female. Some who cannot see or hear in the spirit world, can feel the spirits, or at least feel the vibration that lets them know that spirits are present.

God created the material and spirit world with specific balances of interaction between the two. Both high and low minded humans and spirits must follow those same laws of creation in order to reach one another, whether for good or evil purposes. If we more fully understand the perfection of the laws of spirit communication, it is easier to recognize that the spirit world already influences us in our daily lives. To begin to separate the two and know when the thoughts are our own and when the thoughts are from other sources in the spirit world, we might be able to more easily move through life with fewer mistaken paths. By listening to the quiet voices behind our lives, we can begin to recognize the higher spirits and separate them from the lower and more unwise, possibly even negative spirits, that inhabit the invisible world around us. If we learn the rules, we can learn to move with higher and more pure spiritual influences more often.

We mortals seem to assume that only the world of matter is subject to laws, but God is a God of systems and of laws in all creation, material and spiritual. In His doings He observes the laws which He himself made and disregards none of them. All material creatures and all spirits must observe these whenever one or the other wishes to communicate with the other. People are in the habit of calling many things that happen in the world a 'miracle' until the process of the set laws of God are understood in that vernacular.

MIRACLES

There really is no such thing as a "miracle" according to the meaning placed on that word as coming from nowhere and having no means of explanation. Everything happens according to the same immutable laws, not one of which supersedes or conflicts with another. If we raise a stone, the law of gravity isn't turned off because we intervened, but gravity has been overcome by a greater force like muscle, which opposes the pull of gravity enough to pick the stone off the ground. We see the physical hand and so we know that there is no miracle involved, it was work done by someone to move the stone. If however, a stone were raised by a hand invisible to us, we would consider this to be a miracle because we do not see the force. We might think the stone was rising of its own volition or by some mysterious power, possibly even telepathic levitation. And yet there still must be some law of science which explains the force that causes the stone to be lifted up, even if we don't understand that force because we can't see it or conceive of it.

There is a story of levitation in the Old Testament with the prophet Elisha (2 Kings 6:1-7). The young prophets who were studying under him had gone to cut trees near the Jordan

River to build a new lodging for themselves, having outgrown the old one as their numbers increased. One of the student's ax head flew off its handle and into the muddy river. Elisha threw a stick into the river and the metal ax head floated up to the top of the water. The heavy ax head could not have lifted up unless a force, such as an invisible hand of an angel (spirit) had picked it up for the young men, to prove to them God's willingness to help them accomplish good goals in their lives.

Whenever anything happens that is out of the realm of human understanding, we call it a miracle. If we could see what transpires, we would understand that there really are no miracles. God created everything by setting up laws that do not ever change and even God observes His own laws. Humanity is not cognizant of all of God's laws, but our ignorance of God's laws does not mean they do not exist. In past ages people believed the earth was flat and that the sun moved around the earth, now we would laugh at someone who still believed this, so why is it acceptable to believe that we have discovered all of nature's laws which are God's laws. When we understand how communication works, we realize that there are no miracles, all of these things have an explanation and all of them do not defy science since God created the laws of science, or His own laws. Mankind has adopted God's laws for their own in the governing of their countries, and many who say they do not believe in God still follow these rules or defy them at their own peril.

There is nothing 'miraculous' in the fact that the spirit-world should communicate and speak with mankind. Whenever God's spirits speak to us they do so according to fixed laws which they are bound to observe, and which would have to be observed equally by any evil spirit which might desire to speak to us. When we compare this to our telephone, there are many of nature's laws which we must comply with before we can use these for speaking. We must have a current, wires and other parts to transmit speech and adapted to the laws of acoustics and electricity, and these laws apply whether the phone is used by a good citizen or by a criminal.

Communication between the spiritual world and the material world happens all the time, but to various degrees. Some people barely sense that there are spirits around or what the spirits tell them, in an entirely instinctive way, while others have greater cognizance of their guidance. The so-called mediums have these natural abilities highly developed and are able to communicate with the spirits and interact with them by several means, listening, seeing, writing. Direct manipulation of physical objects by spirits is also possible., however, for it to happen the spirits need the help (voluntary or not) of the ethereal energy received from material sources. The source can be plants, animals, the earth itself, or from human mediums with particular abilities for physical effects.

Communication with the spirits is often called spiritualism or spiritism, and there are many critics who describe it as charlatanism, pseudoscience, heresy, anti-Christian, witchcraft and even Satanism. Today many churches misunderstand the spiritual meanings found in the Bible. For example, in the NIV Bible, God tells Moses that all mediums and spiritists must be put to death, whereas the King James Bible says that God tells Moses that all those who have familiar spirits and wizards must be put to death. There is big difference between these versions. Familiar spirits and wizards were witches, those who communicated with low spirits only. But rules of contact between the spirit and the flesh are the same for both high and low spirits even to this day. When God commanded that the Hebrews were to not consult the low spirit realm and gods of other tribes, He said, "Inquire of me, ask me of things to come concerning my sons, and concerning the works of my hands ".(Isaiah 5:1)

Those who reject spirit communication fail to realize that the Bible is a collection of works which is almost entirely based on spirit communication, so if you believe in the Bible, you believe in spirit communication. The four gospels in the New Testament are claimed to be the inspired word of God while all of the miracles performed by Jesus, the apostles, and the Old Testament prophets, are proof positive of the interaction between spirits and physical beings. Not only that, but Jesus promised that everyone could work towards the same communication that He possessed. Jesus promised to send the spirits of truth to His followers.

In Biblical days most understood spirit communication, it was not something out of the ordinary. The good prophets or seers were forever passing on messages from God's kingdom warning people not to communicate with the lower or evil spirits, it was called idolatry, or adultery or harlotry.

In the New Testament, Paul speaking to the Corinthians says, "Now we have not received one of the evil spirits that rule the world, but a spirit that comes from God, thus we deliver the spirit's message in the same words in which the spirit gave it to us. True, a worldly-minded man does not accept what comes from a spirit of God, for he looks upon communication with God's spirit-world as madness. Neither is he fit to understand it correctly, for only those who know the laws governing spirit communication can properly judge it" (Cor 2:12-15).

Not much has changed, those who would reject and ridicule spirit communication are those who have no idea how the process works, and yet they set themselves up to be the judge of such things of which they know nothing.

ENERGY OR OD

In the mid 1800's Baron Karl Von Reichenbach opened a whole vista of new knowledge when he discovered the existence and properties of what he called "Od force", a force that flows from minerals and light, in plants and animals, and even radiates from the stars. The Od or Odic force, named for the Norse god Odin, is a mysterious force that permeates all things, that is everywhere present, and surely must be easily revealed, but is not consciously perceptible to most.

Rudolph Steiner believed that all human beings had senses that could perceive the ether, and that, especially through initiation and mental discipline, these senses could be awakened. He believed that the mind may be trained to see subtle forces, like the Odic force.

All life in both the material world and in the world of spirit is bound up with this odic force. This is the most powerful force in creation, and it is the force by means of which God, who is the source of this force, can overthrow all things, and the means by which He and his spirit world perform the greatest 'miracles' as we call them. It is the force which renders the Magician capable of superhuman performances, inasmuch as his own powers are increased by the spirit world, whether the good or the evil, depending on which of the two he is in communication with.

The way that humankind can communicate with spirits is by the use of this energy, or "life force" or "od force". God creates the conditions by which we can communicate with Him or with His angels or spirits. Since everything contains energy, He can draw upon this energy and use it in whatever method He wishes, all we have to do is follow the laws that He has created. One of those laws is the ability to condense and expand energy or od.

10

We can use the example of changes in water. When the sun heats a body of water, the water evaporates and becomes a cloud until it is cooled off and falls back to earth in a more condensed form, called rain, with extra condensation, it becomes a solid that we call ice. In a similar manner, the matter which makes up our body can be de-materialized and can be condensed to appear as a cloud and re-condensed into matter. We all understand the laws governing evaporation and condensation, evaporation requires hot currents while condensation requires cold currents.

According to Johannes Greber's book, "Communication With the Spirit World of God", all bodies of terrestrial beings are condensed od or energy derived from the odic radiation of the earth and that of its surrounding heavenly bodies. The body, therefore, is nothing but od condensed into substance, and this is true of all bodies, not only those of human beings, but those of animals, plants and minerals. The od of individual material organisms represents a mixture of od of the most varied strength and kinds, produced by wonderful laws unknown to man. Their growth and their taking material shape are subject to those self-same laws of odic condensation.

In man this mixture is different from that found in animals, different from that found in plants, different from that found in minerals. The difference obtains not only between the primary groups of Nature, but between individual organisms within the same group. The odic composition of the various human races differs and not all members of the same race have the same odic composition, and every individual has his own odic composition, which is not the same in any two human beings, and the same thing applies to animals, plants and minerals.

At the death of terrestrial bodies the odic force remains vested in the spirit, for those bodies possess no independent energy force of their own, it is only the spirits which have taken possession of the bodies which have that power. The words" "Of earth thou art, to earth shalt thou return", therefore apply to all terrestrial things.

Everything that has life has energy or od, every person, animal, plant and heavenly body. There is energy in water, air, fire and earth. .

There is od or energy in all terrestrial bodies and it radiates beyond them to a certain distance that we call an 'aura' and which some people can see. We often see pictures of some we think are holy with a halo around their heads, could it be that someone who was clairvoyant had seen the aura around the heads of others to draw such a picture.

ENERGY TRANSMISSION

We transmit energy from one living thing to another. We take the energy from the plants we eat, and we use the energy of plants, beasts and minerals as remedies for our own ailments. The heavenly bodies as well as the earth give us energy. People take energy from each other; a mother gives energy to her sick child as she comforts it, and the child feels better. An ill person will heal faster if friends visit because they transmit energy to the ill person. A healthy person who sleeps with old or sick people for any great length of time takes on a sickly appearance while the sick person feels better, and for this reason children should not be allowed to sleep in the same bed with old people.

When King David was old and sick, he was unable to keep warm and a young girl was sent to take care of him to keep him warm, " So they sought for a fair damsel throughout all the coasts of Israel and found Abishag, a Shunamite and brought her to the king" (Kings 1-4). Abishag was not just any young girl, she was a medium or prophet who could use her energy to heal and comfort King David.

We also transmit energy or od to everything we touch. A clairsentient person can feel the energy from an item owned by someone and tell us about the owner. A sensitive person is sometimes uncomfortable wearing second hand clothing or owning second hand items because of the energy of the original owner. We often feel attracted to people or repelled by their presence all because we can feel the energy or vibration of that other person. A dog can follow the energy of a lost person by familiarizing himself with the energy of that person. Birds can return to their nesting place by following their own energy. Our energy produces a trail from the beginning of our life to the end of it, like a person carrying a bag of sand with a hole in the bag; wherever the person goes, it can be traced. If this is the criteria for the eventual decision for the life of our spirit after death, there is no room for error.

When someone is healed by the touch of a hand, they sometimes can feel the energy from the person's hand, it feels like electricity or heat. Some so-called healers can sometimes give their od to invigorate a weak person and induce healing, and God may allow angels to heal people, such as we read all through the Bible, and especially with His son Jesus Christ. Because Christ was given the most important mission to save all mankind, great power was given to him to manifest God's power to mankind. Christ's own mediumistic healing ability was the greatest possible because he is the greatest of spirits created by God.

The extent to which the spirit of a person can infuse strength into his physical energy through the spirit's own power and by the exercise of his will power, can be observed in life in many forms. The physical energy force of paralyzed persons, threatened with great danger, often receives a sufficient amount of energy through the will power of their spirit to restore to them the use of their limbs, temporarily at least. This same effect is produced by a patient's firm expectation of getting well. Will power expressed in courage, hope, faith and cheerfulness is the best remedy and is the best safeguard against contagious diseases. Lack of will power and of courage, fear and timidity have the opposite effect. Free will is the greatest gift God could have bestowed on His children, and this requires us to be engaged in every thought, decision and action that we deem to choose.

Jesus did not heal everyone, but only those whom God decided should be healed because of their good character or their possibility of improving. When someone is healed, the healing may not last if the person does not have a change of heart and continues in his present attitude. Most of the healing done by Jesus was to prove the power of God to the people. After each healing, Jesus would say, "Go and sin no more", which leads us to believe that the person's attitude was important in their healing.

The apostles also were in communication with God's spirits and were enabled by them to perform healing among the people. It is usually difficult to convince people of your message unless they see some miracle to attract their attention, just as we use a brightly colored object to get a child's attention before we can teach them something.

There are many clergymen who hold crusades where they preach and experience healing among the crowd. I have been privileged to attend one of these meetings with the Pastor Benny Hinn. On that particular day, a child who was deaf was healed as well as some who could not walk. I cannot prove to you more than I could see for myself, but he seems to see by clairvoyance and announces the healings as they occur. Everyone in the audience were holding their hands in the air and so I decided to do the same to find out what the reason was, and I felt a great deal of electricity in the air radiating around my hands. Therefore, I think that a lot of energy the holy spirits used to heal was taken from the people in the crowd as well as from Benny Hinn.

In recent times, Reinhard Bonnke, an evangelist, born in 1940 in Germany, is known for his great gospel crusades in Africa. At the time of this writing, he is still active and is privileged to see the most amazing healings.   His crowds number up to a million people at a time and the crusades must be held outdoors to accommodate everyone.

When we see the videos of the crusades that Rev Bonnke holds, there are many people leaving wheelchairs and people healed from deafness and other health problem. There is one occurrence of a mother who brought her newborn to Rev Bonnke after the first day of the crusade and showed him that the child had no eyes. The next day she returned to the crusade and showed how there seemed to be a couple of marble sized balls under the skin where the child's eyes would be. Then on the third day, she showed the baby with completely formed eyes and eyelids.   This phenomenon is often experienced in such crusades.

THE ODIC CORD

When a person has an out of body experience, the spirit leaves the body but it eventually returns because it is attached to the body by a band of energy or od, sometimes called a cord of energy, or a silver cord (eccl 12:6). When people die, this cord is broken and can never be re-attached. The only way for the person to return to physical life is to temporarily materialize or reincarnate in a body by birth.   All of the stories we hear of people who were really ill, died and returned to life are not the fulfillment of permanent death and the breaking of the odic silver cord. They did not entirely die, but their spirit left their body and returned. It does not matter how long they were gone, their energy cord had not broken. Doctors do not really know when the silver cord breaks, but they decide by our lack of brain waves that we are too weak to return to our former self.   From the time that a person is said to be dead to the time that the silver cord breaks might be instant or several days.

14

In the account in the New Testament of Lazarus being restored to life even after he was wrapped in burial clothes and entombed, it was the Divine Spirit world which restored all energy and repaired all organs necessary to reanimate Lazarus in his human body. His odic cord connecting his spirit to his body was not entirely disconnected. Jesus made this known to his disciples when he said, "Our friend Lazarus is asleep" (John 11:11) although he appeared to everyone else as dead. But since the people didn't understand what Jesus meant, he finally said "Lazarus is dead" (John 11:14) only to put an end to the conversation at that time.

One of the most remarkable stories is regarding a young woman in Nigeria whose husband, Daniel, was in a motorcycle accident and after being checked by two different doctors was pronounced dead and taken to the morgue. After three days in the morgue, the woman decided that since God can do anything, there was no reason why He could not return her husband to her, so she had her friends take her husband out of the morgue and returned to her village. Then she had them take him to a crusade in a building where Reinhard Bonnke was preaching. They were not allowed to take the dead man into the hall so she placed him in an adjoining room and they all prayed for him. After some time that same day, her husband was returned to his full capacity. He returned to his village to see his father and to greet all of his friends and neighbors.

If these people had faith in God before this, you can imagine the faith they had after this occurrence. We know that this man was not really dead because the energy cord was not broken, otherwise he could not have returned to life, but it would have taken a great deal of mediumistic power from Clergyman Bonnke to have this result. The story is known as the Lazarus story, and for good reason. Jesus did say that anyone who believed could do what he did and more.

Rev Reinhard Bonnke has also held crusades in America, but is particularly known for his African visits. He claims that he sees life in pictures. When evangelists are asked why the people of Africa and similar countries seem to have so much more faith than those in more developed countries, we are told that they believe in spirits, good and bad, so it is not a long trip to believe that a God Who is this powerful can create such miracles.

We, in so-called more enlightened countries, have much more work to do in order to understand and act in the manner that Jesus and his apostles did, because the churches have forbidden all communication with the spirit world for so long that most do not even know how to hone our skills so that we can communicate with the spirits They teach that all spirit communication can only be with the evil spirits. They give no credit to God for His ability to communicate with man. Could it be that if we all learned to communicate directly with God's spirits some would suddenly find themselves unemployed? Many Christian churches do not recognize that their whole belief system is based on the Bible which is almost completely based on spirit communication.

Most churches today teach that Jesus after his death returned to physical life, as a physical resurrection. Jesus' spirit was permanently released from his physical body. The band of energy was broken never to be re-connected, so he could not have returned to physical life, "Or ever the silver cord be loosed" (Eccl 12:6). But Jesus did materialize several times and appeared to hundreds of his disciples after his crucifixion and death and disappearance from the tomb. Eventually he de-materialized and returned to Heaven. The words "life and death" in the Bible usually mean spiritual life and death. Spiritual life is life with God and spiritual death means living without God as when the word death is used to describe Satan, the angel of death. Jesus had descended to the lower spheres which are the spheres of the dead, or hell, and then returned to the higher realms, the realms of the living in Heaven.

In the Bible, Jesus is sometimes reported as being non-physical, "being put to death in the flesh, quickened by the Spirit", (1 Peter 3:18). Then sometimes he is portrayed as being physical, "Behold my hands and feet, that it is I myself...." (Luke 24:39). It would make more sense that he had died and was materializing and that was why his followers did not always recognize him until they heard his voice. "And when she (*Mary*) had thus said, she turned herself back, and saw Jesus standing and knew not that it was Jesus" (John 20:14).

INQUIRING OF THE DEAD

The world of God's spirits has been excluded from the Christian churches. The leaders of the churches have "extinguished the holy spirits". However, wherever God's spirits are forced to give ground, others appear, the very ones of which Paul writes to Timothy, "God's spirit world expressly declares that in later times, many will fall away from the true faith turning to spirits of deceit, and spreading doctrines inspired by demons" (Tim 4:1-2). Today we have a Christianity split asunder into countless sects, each preaching many things that are not true, and each believing its own creed to be the one and only true gospel of Christ.

The churches tell us that the Bible warns us against 'inquiring of the dead'. This does not mean that we are not to inquire of anyone who does not have a physical body, inquiring of the dead means those who are spiritually dead, the low and evil spirits who are in the world of Lucifer, who is called "death". In (Isaiah 8:19) God says "Why consult the dead on behalf of the living". If the Bible were speaking of the physically dead, then we must realize that God does not have a physical body either.

Moses when he was saying goodbye to the Israelites before his death, told the people. "See, I have set before thee this day life and good, death and evil", (Deut 30 :15). Moses did not mean that they could remain physically alive forever but that they could have spiritual life.

Before Jesus died he told his disciples that he had to leave in order that he could send them the holy spirits to teach them the things that they could not yet understand and to remind them of all the things he had taught them. His plan was not that people should create religions and teach from their own store of knowledge, but that the leaders should communicate with the good spirits and use this information to teach. He himself never tired of telling people that he did not teach on his own but only taught what his Father in Heaven, through the holy spirits, told him to teach. God's spirits are the sole source of the truth, this is the legacy that Jesus bequeathed to us in his last hours.

Some churches practice what they call "moved by the spirit", by which a spirit speaks through someone which they call "speaking in tongues". They believe that this is 'the holy spirit' speaking through the person and is to be much desired. Paul encouraged his congregations to practice speaking in tongues only if there were someone who could translate that language so that everyone could understand, since speaking a foreign language did nothing to enlighten the people if there were no people present who understood the foreign language. The churches believe that there is only one holy spirit, "the holy spirit", but there are many holy spirits and there are also many low or evil spirits. Speaking in tongues is not proof that holy spirits are communicating, but only proof that spirits of any type can communicate through people. Depending on the character of the churches and of its people, any kind of spirit could be speaking through mediums, and if they are speaking in a language unknown to the congregation, how do they know what these spirits are saying? These gifted people would be such a blessing to their churches if they could practice letting the good spirits speak in the language of the congregation.

During Biblical days, many knew the rules of communicating with spirits. God was forever sending messages through His prophets warning against communicating with low or evil spirits. Once people were in the habit of communicating with the evil spirits, their obsessions prevented them from ending the practice. They looked at their idols as gods since evil spirits used these idols to create all kinds of extraordinary effects. Once the people were taken in by these spirits they were enticed to even sacrifice their children to these idols and to commit all kinds of heinous crimes, and they seemed powerless to walk away from these spirits.

This idol worship was a backward step for the Israelites. God had allowed them a material body to help them progress on this earth in order to return to Heaven, but now they were returning to their roots. Having been given a chance to learn about the true God, they were returning to their worship of idols. It might be a long time before they could incarnate on earth again to remove their character flaws. There is a war on this earth between good and evil for the minds of mankind and we are allowed to choose a side once more as we were allowed to while in Heaven; we can choose to follow Jesus and return to Heaven or we can choose to keep following Lucifer and remain at the lower levels, or even go down to a lower level than we already are. Many people regret the bad choices they made on earth once they return to the spirit world. The Bible talks of salt as a metaphor to cleanse one's soul by purification, burning out all impurities in life just as salt can be painful if it is applied to a wound, in the end, will also heal the wound. By exposing mankind to his or her character flaws even though it might be painful, will in the end prove to be the best way to cause a change in each person. In the story of the destruction of Sodom and Gomorrah, the Bible says that Lot's wife turned into a pillar of salt when she returned to her old lifestyle of debauchery. This explains the degree of sorrow and regret she encountered once she returned to the spirit world.

When Moses was on Mount Sinai, the people grew impatient and had Aaron make them a golden calf which they worshiped. Then Moses, " took the calf and burnt it in the fire, and ground it to powder and strawed it upon the water and made the children of Israel drink of it" (Ex 32:20). It is well known that gold has a purifying quality and Moses was guided by the good spirit world to do this to increase the vibration by pure od sources to break the hold of evil spirits over them, as a last effort to bring them back to their senses and to lead the people away from the dark path they were following. It was to purify the people who had contaminated themselves by worshiping their idol. There is a nutritional supplement called 'colloidal gold' that some people take to improve their memory. It is claimed to be useful in helping those who have had concussions as well.

Of all the minerals, gold has a great value because it does not deteriorate, does not rust, oxidize or mix over time with impurities in the atmosphere. It is malleable, is a great conducter of energy, and as mentioned, also has healing properties when applied to the human body in the correct form. When the Bible talks about God guiding His creation to a continual path to greater purity of character and spirit, the message in the Bible compares it to purifying gold in a hot furnace, "Behold I have refined thee as silver ....". So also, it may seem like a fiery event to change habits and to adopt a more pure character, in the end the spirit once purified can now be counted as more valuable for greater purposes wherein God can guide each person..

THE ODIC CLOUD

When God, or an angel that He sends, speaks to someone in the physical world, as He did with Abraham, He cannot be heard unless He uses the energy of the earth to condense His speech or His vocal chords to be heard in the physical creation. These laws of spirit communication from Heaven is mentioned when God utilized His laws of creation for Abraham to hear. "When the sun went down and it was dark, behold a smoking furnace, and a burning lamp that passed between those pieces" (Gen 15:17). The odic current, when only slightly condensed, looks like a cloud of smoke and has a reddish-yellow gleam in the dark, like the flame of fire.

In the story of Moses, God called him to go back to Egypt to rescue His people while Moses was living in his new land of Midian after running away from Egypt. Moses saw a burning bush and heard the voice of the spirit or angel, "..the bush burned with fire, and the bush was not consumed" (Ex 3:2).

The bush was not really burning, it was glowing. This tells us that the angel appeared at night. Had it been daylight, it would have looked like a cloud. Again the angel was not fully formed and Moses could only see the energy of the partial materialization.

When God sent an angel to lead Moses and the people out of Egypt, "And the Lord went before them by day in a pillar of cloud, to lead them the way, and by night in a pillar of fire, to give them light; to go by day and night"(Ex 13:21). It was not necessary for the angel to completely materialize, all that was necessary was to partially condense the angel's ethereal body and let the people follow. When energy is only partially condensed, it appears as a cloud in the daytime and as a light or fire in the dark. God used the energy of the earth and everything on the earth to condense the pillar of cloud and fire. It would have taken more energy to have the angel appear completely but it was not necessary, and God does not waste energy when the right amount will suffice.

When God wished to speak to Moses and the people, on Mount Sinai, He gave specific instructions regarding what would take place. He told Moses that in order for the people to hear Him, He would cover the mountain in a huge cloud. The denser the cloud, the louder the sound. The same is true of our radio, the stronger the current, the clearer the sound.

www.bible.ca

Moses had to warn the people not to go near the mountain while the cloud was forming and that if anyone, man or beast, came too near the mountain they would die. "Whosoever toucheth the mount shall be surely put to death (Ex 19:12). God was not threatening the people with death if they disobeyed, if so, what about the animals, why would God punish them, they did not understand what was going on. God was not threatening to punish the people, He was looking after their safety. In order for the material world to hear the voice of God, the holy spirits in charge of the job called Cherubim or chemists, had to use the laws of materialization of matter to condense that voice.

The clouds were the condensation of that energy. Just as rain clouds release electricity in the form of lightning as they condense which we see when it grounds to the earth, so also the condensed energy which God used to communicate with His servants also released electric energy as it condensed. During the condensation of the energy, it was not safe for any creature to be near or they would act as a lighting rod grounded to the earth. Once the cloud had formed, the current was shut off and it was safe for the people to advance toward the mountain. From the dense cloud, the people could hear the voice of God and they were terrified, this was all so new to them. When God required anyone to approach the current, as He did with Moses, He provided insulation to keep him safe, just as we use insulation to protect ourselves from electrical currents here on earth. The cloth that covered Moses' face, was required of Moses when he went up the mountain to meet with God.

When Jesus appeared to Mary Magdalene after his death on the cross, the Bible quotes Jesus as saying, "Do not touch me! I have not yet ascended to the Father" (John 20:17). This cannot be the reason for not touching him, as he appeared to the apostles and allowed Thomas to touch him although he had not yet ascended to the Father. To understand this quote you need to understand that he was just in the process of materializing, and had Mary touched him at that time, it would have interfered with the materialization and caused harm to Mary.

The same effect was present when Jesus de-materialized before his apostles. At the final exit by Jesus after his victory over Lucifer, he disappeared in brilliant "clouds of glory", by de-materializing into the spirit world and back to his throne in Heaven at the right hand of God. "When he had spoken these words a cloud suddenly enveloped him from his feet to his head, and he was thereby withdrawn from their sight (Acts 1:9).

Jesus was not hiding behind a cloud in order to disappear, he was the cloud that was created by his de-materialization.

On the day of Pentecost, a great gust of wind was heard and above the heads of each of the disciples, "Tongues as of fire appeared before them, and dividing, settled on each one present. Every one was filled with a holy spirit and began to speak in foreign languages whatever the spirit prompted him to utter" (Acts 2:3). By the fact that the energy or od looked like flames tells us that this happened at night, possibly around one o'clock in the morning.

This is an example of the fact that there are many holy spirits or angels, and in this case each disciple fell into a trance and experienced an individual Heavenly spirit which spoke through them in a particular language, so that the onlookers could each hear their own language. The phrase, "the holy spirit" as used by the churches teaches that there is only one holy spirit and that it is an entity unto itself. The term "the holy spirit" is a collective noun, just as when we say, " I will get the doctor", does not mean that there is only one doctor.

The people in the Bible, who were still communicating with the low spirits, set up their places of worship and also burned sacrifices to create the odic currents. It says in the Bible that they sacrificed under trees and in shady places. The people did this because in order to communicate with any spirit by a human, whether that spirit is a pure spirit from Heaven or is a low and evil spirit from lower realms, the same rules of spirit communication apply. They worshiped in cool and shady places because cool places are more conducive to communication. Scientists often ridicule those who hold seances in the dark, believing that the dark allows for sleight of hand. But apparitions are more easily seen when it is dark and cool, as heat and light dissipates the energy. It would be as foolish to ask a photographer to develop his pictures in the light. Communication with low spirits uses the same methods as that to communicate with the high spirits, just as a telephone can be used for good or evil.

When the Israelites won a war, they were often told to destroy everything in that area, including all the evil people, their children who had begun to follow that same path, the plants that had been dedicated to the evil spirit world, even all the animals of that same infected village, just as a plague can only be stopped by burning everything infected by that disease today. This seems like a drastic measure, but it was because the people in that area were sacrificing to idols, which are evil spirits. This practice contaminates all of the people and everything they are in contact with. God did not want any of this contamination to touch His people, the Israelites. He didn't want His people to be taken over by the low and evil spirits, for then He would need to begin all over again, raising another group of people whom He could teach in order to raise the character of the known world. Mankind being closer to the control of low realms than in higher realms, is susceptible to both physical as well as mental diseases of character and mind. In the time of the ancient Israelites, it was much more compelling to pay attention to these evil spirits because they could actually see and hear them, since continual communication strengthened their mediumistic abilities.

THE ARK OF THE COVENANT

In the days of Moses, God gave the Israelites the "Tent of Testimony" in order to help them abandon the worship of idols. In the tent of testimony, was the "Ark of the Covenant" that Moses built according to God's instructions. There are many opinions regarding the use of this ark. Most people think that the ark was only a type of box to hold the tablets with the ten commandments, a pot of manna and Aaron's budded rod.

Ark of the Covenant

The ark likely contained all of these articles but it had a much more important purpose. God said to Moses, "There I will meet with thee and I will commune with thee from above the mercy seat from between the two cherubim which are upon the Ark of Testimony of all things which I will give thee in commandment unto the children of Israel", (Ex 25:22). This doesn't sound like God only wanted the children of Israel to have a container for the sacred objects but to use it to communicate with Moses and His people.

The ark was to be covered in gold and only built with the purest of materials so that there would be no contamination from impure energy sources. Among the minerals, gold, silver and copper possess the purest mineral odic mixture, as shown by the fact that they do not rust. For rust collects by the absorption of impure od, which has a destructive effect on any other od into which it penetrates. Also the top of the ark had carvings of two cherubim whose wings touched each other, to contain the energy just as the burning bush held the energy. With this energy, the Lord could make Himself heard. In Exodus 33:11, it says this very thing; "The Lord would speak to Moses face to face, as one speaks to a friend". This phenomena is called "direct voice", where they could hear the exact words spoken by the angel. As we know, anytime that a human is used to communicate with spirits, there is always a chance for error. God wanted to communicate directly with the people thereby bypassing humans altogether. He also wanted to communicate with the Israelites on a daily basis, and just as God required that we strive in all things, so also He wanted the people to supply as much energy on their own, without needing to use energy brought by Holy spirits.

Terrestrial beings are carriers of terrestrial od, and since the energy of the material world is a complex mixture of varieties of od taken from all over the earth; the od required to enable God to speak with men was drawn from a great variety of earthly sources, including minerals, plants, herbs, oil, wine and animals.

A very important requirement was the preparation of the od itself which would be used by the Heavenly spirits to create the materialization, and was seen floating as a cloud above the ark. This was required for the production of the sounds by which God spoke to Moses. The spirit sounds were condensed by the terrestrial od of the cloud to the extent necessary to make them audible to human ears. As the Bible says; "And when

Moses entered the Trysting tent to speak to Him, he heard the voice speaking to him from above the cover on the ark of the presence, between the two cherubs: and the Eternal said to him...... ".

The people burned parts of animals plus grains, oils etc. to produce the cloud of energy through which the Lord could speak. Only certain parts of the animal were used, those parts that produced the purest od. When the ark of the covenant trapped the partly materialized energy sources from the burning sacrifices, the person who stood nearby could hear the message that God wished to impart to the people. A similar case of de-materialization of energy sources and re-materialization happens today in another way by the digestion of food we eat, breaking the individual molecules down to their simplest state where they are guided by sophisticated systems in our bodies to create the various organs and substances that make up our bodies.

Aaron and his sons would be the only ones allowed where the energy was collected. They had to be clean and wear only garments that were of the purest fabric so as not to contaminate the area. When Aaron's sons died for not following the instructions, again, it was not that God wanted to punish them, it was that they did not follow the rules to protect themselves from the powerful currents forming at that moment.

The animals for the sacrifices had to be only those whose od was of the purest. The beasts called unclean in the Bible are those having the lowest and most impure od of any creatures whose flesh could not conceivably serve for human food. That also is the reason why the people were forbidden to eat the flesh of unclean animals. For instance, the flesh of swine is not to be recommended as an article of diet, particularly for growing children. What we call scrofula would scarcely be found among children if they were denied the flesh of swine, which is not wholesome even for adults if it forms a substantial part of the daily diet. The animals must also be without flaws or disease since holy spirits cannot use impure energy being pure beings themselves. It seems interesting to note that the demons in (Mark 5:12) asked Jesus to let them enter the bodies of the swine rather than to send them away.

I   In movies of Bible stories, the writers do not understand the meaning of the need for the purest of animals for sacrifices. They explain it by saying that the Israelites had to give up their most prized possessions in order to prove their love for God, but this is not so. The od from the burning sacrifices created the conditions for them to be able to communicate with God directly or through His angels or spirits, and if the od was not pure, they could not communicate with God's spirits but only with the lower ones.

When Solomon built the temple to house the Ark of the Covenant, there were huge caverns adjacent to the temple. Some archaeologists speculated that these held water for cleansing but there is also the theory that they were used as Odic baffles to store de-materialized od. This source was similar to a battery storage for long term materialization and direct voice even after all odic sources of animals, plants, spices, herbs and such were already burned up in the preparation for direct voice materialization.

The brilliance of the clouds from where God's spirits manifested are indicative of the brilliance of the spirits. Similar accounts of materialization of low spirits often describe, not only a stench, but a cloud of darkness which comparatively is indicative of low spirit impurities and a negative attitude toward God, who is the source of light, life and purity.

After Moses died and Joshua became the leader of the Israelites, God used the Ark of the Covenant to establish Joshua as leader for the Hebrew people. He caused the waters of the Jordan River to recede so the Israelites could walk across on dry land just as He had done for Moses in the Red Sea. As soon as the Levites stepped into the river carrying the Ark of the Covenant, the waters were held back and the people walked across. When the Levites stepped out of the river on the other side, the waters returned (Joshua 3:17).

Once they had arrived on the other side of the river into the land of Canaan, the people ate the last of their stores of food and there was no more manna given to them, but they were able to eat of the food that grew in that area because this was the land of milk and honey that God has promised them.

MEDIUMS
TYPES OF MEDIUMS

When anyone saw an angel as related in the Bible, that spirit used the energy of the earth or of the people who were to see the angel manifest to them. This brings us to another related topic. People use their energy for all of their activities and most people's energy is closely attached to them. However, there are some who can release their energy to communicate with the spirit world. One need only concentrate his or her efforts in releasing that energy, usually by focused meditation. Those who have the ability to release their energy for spirit communication, we call mediums. They are only a catalyst or an instrument to create the energy. Such were the people of the Bible that we read about: Abraham, Isaac, Jacob, Joseph, and Mary plus the priests and prophets. It was their faithfulness and pure character that blocked the negative spirits and allowed them to receive guidance from holy spirits.

We learn that there were schools of prophets where people could go to learn how to become mediums. The meaning of the term,"prophet" in the Bible does not mean those who could foretell the future, although they might also been given a look at future events, but that they were mediums or psychics. The most important requirement in these schools for prophets was a clean and pure heart.

The requirement to communicate with spirits is connected with the ability to release our energy or od for the spirits to use, or to supply pure od sources such as the purest of Biblical essential oils such a frankincense, myrrh, galbanum and others, or for a person's spirit to separate from its physical body and to see into the spirit world. There are many who can communicate with spirits but not many who are able to communicate with the higher spirits. A large portion of psychics or mediums reach only the same level as themselves or a lower spirit level than themselves because of the lifestyle they live and their interests. These type of spirits know little of the steps to take to refine one's soul to go to Heaven after physical death. The psychics do not need as much practice to become a medium for lower spirits, because these lower spirits do not need pure od or pure energy to communicate, they can communicate with impure energy that is of a similar type as the spirits who use it. They communicate messages that relate only to the material world, that of money, love and states of physical life.

In order to communicate with the higher spirits, there are greater requirements of character development and purity of energy sources. The communicator must have a much purer type of energy so they can meet the high spirits partway. Our thoughts are influenced by spirits who think as we do. If we are totally involved in the material world, those are the type of spirits who accompany us. People who strive to constantly refine their character are more easily reached by spirits who come from a higher realm. In the Old Testament, God even gave rules of diet and lifestyle that would assist the Israelite in reaching the purest spirits.

WRITING MEDIUMS

Mediums are of different types depending on how they are used by the spirit world. Some are writing mediums; of those there are some who are inspirational mediums. Their thoughts are inspired by a spirit and they write them down. Most of the writings of the apostles, in the New Testament, were written in this way.

Another's hand may be guided at the same time that the words he writes are inspired into his mind. All the while he is fully conscious of his actions. Contemporaneous inspiration is necessary in those cases in which the medium offers strong resistance to the guidance of his hand.

Others again know only that they are writing, but are quite ignorant of what they set down.

Still others write in a state .of utter unconsciousness; they know neither that they are writing nor what they are writing. It not infrequently happens that one and the same medium will write in several of these ways.

THE BREASTPLATE OF JUDGMENT

There is another class of mediums, namely the 'planchette mediums'. A 'planchette' is a slab of wood, metal or other material upon which are marked the letters of the alphabet, figures and other symbols. The surface of the planchette is smooth, so that an object may readily be slid about upon it. The medium, who retains his full consciousness, lays his hand on some object with a pointer which rests on the slab. He now waits until the object moves so that the pointer will touch a letter. It indicates, one after another, a series of letters which when put together will spell words and sentences.

The most famous of all planchettes was the 'Breastplate of Judgment'. This was a plate with twelve precious stones, set in a semi-circle, each representing one of the tribes. The planchette was made only of the most pure of materials such as gold and silver and the purest of precious stones. The medium or priest who was assigned to this had to be of the purest character as well.   In Moses' day, Aaron, the high priest, held the breastplate on himself and the pointer in his head dress. The Israelites used it to receive answers from God regarding occurrences in their lives. The stones contained large quantities of the most valuable od.

When the Israelites battled against Jericho, (Joshua 7:1), God told them to destroy everything except the gold, silver, brass and iron, and if anyone took of anything else in Jericho they would make the camp of Israel a curse and trouble it, because of the evil spirits present in the city. Shortly after the destruction of Jericho, Joshua sent his army to defeat the Amorites but the Amorites were winning the war so Joshua realized that someone had brought something out of Jericho to curse them. He then used the Breastplate of Judgment to single out which tribe and which person within that tribe who had taken something.   It was found that Achan had taken a Babylonian garment along with some coins. After these items were destroyed, the Israelites had no trouble winning the war.

When the Danites sought an inheritance to dwell in, they sent five men to spy out the land. These came to the house of Micah where they met a Levite who lived there as a medium. And they said   " Ask counsel , we pray thee, of God, that we may know whether our way which we go shall be prosperous". And the priest said to them, "Go in peace, before Jehovah is your way wherein you go". It is related that Micah had caused a founder to make him a 'graven image' and a 'molten image'. Some assume that these images were idols, but they were made in imitation of the breastplate of judgment worn on the garments of the high priest, and so called because it was used for inquiring of God. Imitations of the High Priest's breastplate of judgment were used whenever the people of Israel consulted the Lord in matters of private interest.

King David inquired of God using the Breastplate of Judgment, his medium or priest was Abiathar.

When the people of Israel wanted a king, God allowed them to have one. Their first king was King Saul. He had difficulty staying true to God and for that reason he ended up with evil spirits guiding him.   On the day before the battle of Gilboa, Saul, who because of his disobedience had been constantly ignored by God's spirits, 'inquired of Jehovah' for his own desires and not God's will.   Jehovah answered him not, neither by 'dreams' (visions) nor by the 'Urim' (The breastplate)

29

nor by the 'prophets'. This indicates that on previous occasions Saul had been answered in one or another of these ways.

OUIJA BOARD

We no longer use the Breastplate of Judgment that God gave to the Israelites, but Lucifer, who is the ruler of this world has provided something similar, as he always tries to copy God's methods. The plate is very similar to the Planchette and is called a Ouija board. It is usually used for fun and games, at least it begins that way. The person operating the board is usually someone who has some mediumistic ability and lends his or her energy to a spirit who moves the pointer on the board. The participants ask questions and the small shape moves on the board pointing to different letters that spell the answer to the question. However, since the players of the Ouija board ask only questions that refer to earthly matters, and questions of no consequence, we can be sure that they are not inquiring of God. Therefore, the ruler of this earthly realm, Lucifer and his spirits are the ones who are answering.

The material that the Ouija board is made from and the impurity of it, more easily allows low spirits as well. God guided the Hebrews to make the holy planchette out of the most pure of materials, thereby further protecting the user from noxious spirits, and even past this, it was God who chose who was to be anointed as priest. God knows the intent of people. Many who believe themselves very good have not passed the tests of character required for direct voice, and for this reason would quickly fall under the subtle deceptions of the evil spirits within a short time.

This is what happened when Gideon placed a planchette in the city for all to inquire of God as they desired. Without a qualified priest to keep the sacred device holy, it quickly fell into the powers of evil as people began to listen to messages of a purely material and selfish interest. People are naturally prone to selfish desires more than those of a pure and holy nature, which is why many people who begin to seek spirit communication might quickly fall to lesser goals offered by the evil spirit world in an attempt to misguide them and keep them from God's great work.

Ego and desire for fame and money and power are promised, and many fall for these deceptions, even before they've passed the first series of tests of character that are required by a human, if they are to serve God. For this reason there were many generations that were denied God's direct voice, it was primarily for their protection and to keep them from becoming even more sinful than they already were. It was God's mercy that He sent His high spirits to influence the Hebrews to turn away from wicked things, impure lifestyles and evil intentions. As the Hebrews grew more aware of their sins and truly had a change of heart, then God reintroduced more means of direct communication with Him. In other generations, only the guardian angels assigned to every person at his or her birth were active in the people's lives with inspirational or automatic writing messages, which were mostly of a personal type, and a means to guide those persons to a good and productive life.

With the Ouija board, the players enjoy this game at first, most of them not understanding how it works. As time goes by, spirit communication becomes stronger and stronger until the operator begins to lose control. Whether or not they continue to use the Ouija board is not relevant after a while. The evil spirits have now found a portal to enter the physical realm and begin to control the operator. Once unleashed, these spirits are not interested in obeying the medium's will but act with their own desires in mind and are difficult to banish. The spirits might even gain enough power to possess the operator and even enter the body of the medium whenever they wish. Not many people in our culture practice exorcism, which is what becomes necessary to rid the person of these spirits, and so the operator might end up in a mental institution. You must remember that the methods to communicate with spirits is the same for good and evil spirits alike, just as a telephone can be used for good or evil.

In Germany, the Brunnen-Gliessen Publishing Co., published a story regarding a protestant clergyman who lived in the nineteenth century and who encountered an experience with a possessed girl by the name of Theophila Dittus. The family had just moved into his parish and there was so much demonic activity in their home that the clergyman Blumhardt was asked to look into it. It appears that Theophila and her sister and brother had been entertaining evil spirits, most likely by using a Ouija board, to the point that Theophila became a full trance medium while the other two were part trance. Clergyman Blumhardt relates the occurrences in this house. Demons had possessed all three of these individuals. The story of demonic activity in the movie "The Exorcist" is a similar fate for those who seek spirit communication without the desire to seek God's will in their lives. It took him two years and many prayers to remove the demons in Theophila's case. After his traumatic experience, he was allowed to work with the good spirit world and received help in healing hearts and lost but seeking souls among the people of his congregation. The story tells how many of the people of his parish felt a compulsion to come to him to repent and he could tell if their sins had been forgiven by an angel assigned to him to say whether God had forgiven that person's sins or not. Although Clergyman Blumhardt had experienced the work of both the evil spirit world and the good spirit world, he never did understand exactly how the spirit world really worked. However, this was not necessary for him to follow the path God had given to him. By his faithfulness to God, he was able to fulfill his life as a servant of God even if all the details of the workings of God were not known to him.

When Jesus was on earth, many brought possessed people to him to have these spirits cast out of them. In today's modern society, people disbelieve in spirit influence and tend to offer explanations of mental incapacity instead. If people today truly understood the importance of a faithful life of prayer, we would surely see more good influence by the angels of Heaven invited, and therefore modern miraculous healing of diseases today. Since there seems to be so few who can cast out the evil or low spirits, we think that we have progressed so much that we are free from this. We believe that what was called possessed in those times were really only mental health problems that were yet unnamed. We have now invented scientific names for this phenomenon, yet the cause may be spirit and not material.

When someone has had so much liquor that he or she loses consciousness and remembers nothing but we notice that their behavior was not typical of their normal behavior, then what occurred? The liquor expelled the spirit of the person and another spirit took its place temporarily, this is a spirit possession. George Ritchie wrote a book called 'Return From Tomorrow', in which he tells of having an out of body experience after suffering from a dangerous illness. In his experience he travels all over town recognizing the streets, then in a drinking establishment he sees a drunk man whose spirit exits his body and another spirit enters him.

More common than spirit possession is spirit obsession. This is where the spirit does not totally invade the body but becomes trapped in a person's aura and is unable or unwilling to leave. It causes the obsessed person to act unlike themselves at times or causes them to have cravings that they cannot seem to control. In all cases, a discarnate spirit who has lost its way and remains on the earth plane is the spirit who obsesses these people. Many of these spirits, if they are at the human level, are at such a low level that they might act and speak in very negative and selfish mannerisms, making the person appear very negative and selfish. Only by striving to correct our own negative and selfish motives and by dedicated prayer to God for guidance can these often mislabeled spirit influences be removed

Carl A. Wickland, M.D. wrote a book in 1974 entitled '30 Years Among the Dead' in which his wife who was very mediumistic, would allow spirits of the dead to enter her, and allow Dr. Wickland to speak to them and attempt to help them understand that they were physically dead and how to move on in their spiritual life. The advice by Dr. Wickland is not always the best one in a truly Godly sense, but the book is a very interesting one, read with a discerning eye, the information is a good challenge to a person seeking to understand this world we live in. All of us have spirits of some type who accompany us in our day, some high, our guardian angel or spirit, some low, of a material and worldly influence, and sometimes some evil, to cause grief or trouble. Depending on our character and progression, will depend on which level has the most influence on us in our lives. It is very rare that anyone reaches the stage in physical life wherein he or she has banished all low spirits from their company. For this reason each person must strive to reach the highest and purest voice, their good conscience, every day and to renew their hope in God daily.

APPORT MEDIUMS

Apport mediums are generally deep trance mediums whose odic force is used by the spirit world to transfer tangible objects into enclosed spaces from without, or from within such space to the outside. The deep trance state is necessary here in most cases, since the spirits require a greater amount of the medium's physical od in order to make these 'apports', as the object apported must be disintegrated into od in one place and re-materialized into substance in the other. These objects might feel hot to the touch at the moment of re-materialization if not enough energy is available to cool the object sufficiently, for although they have been re-condensed by cold currents, they might still retain part of the heat used in their disintegration.

At times a medium's body can be transported from one place to another. This is done by de-materializing it at one spot and re-converting it into substance at the other. When in the Old Testament the prophet Habakuk brought food to Daniel in the lions' den, the angel did not carry Habakuk through the air but de-materialized him and his belongings and re-materialized him at the den.

The same thing happened in the case of the apostle, Philip, after he preached the gospel to and then baptized the eunuch of Queen Candace of Ethiopia, (Acts 8:39) "the spirit of the Lord caught away Philip and carried him to Azotus'. The spirit did not carry Philip through the air but caused him to de-materialize and re-materialize in the city of Azotus.

PHYSICAL MEDIUMS

Another type of medium or prophet, is a physical medium. In the case of a trance medium of this type, the spirits draw from the medium's energy for moving objects, raising tables, chairs and utensils of all kinds. Noises are heard, music is played, drums are beaten, bells ring and objects fly through the room. One name for this type of phenomena is poltergeist. Primarily low or mundane spirits are involved with this type of phenomena. These levels of spirit activity should not be sought out if a person is to remain free from mundane spirit influences in their life. It takes a greater physical force to move physical objects. That energy or odic force comes from a person who is very mediumistic and is able to release much od or energy for spirits to materialize in order to cause the physical phenomena. However, the od or energy alone cannot move objects. Discarnate spirits use it to materialize to such a degree that they can move the objects but not enough that we can see them. These spirits cannot interact with the material world unless they partly materialize their hands so that they can pick up or move objects. No spirit, high or low, can abrogate the laws that are relative to the material world. The good spirits do not primarily manifest with this type of spirit activity. They are not interested in   producing phenomena to gratify man's taste for the extraordinary, but only to guide and increase the faith of those they are sent to minister to.

MATERIALIZATION MEDIUMS

In the book of (1 Kings, 9:5), the Bible says that Elijah battled against the false prophets of Baal. When Elijah was victorious and the Hebrews turned their hearts back to God, and the prophets of Baal were killed, Elijah fled in the wilderness from Jezebel, the wicked queen. In the wilderness, he lay down and slept under a Juniper tree, then an angel touched him and said to him, "arise and eat". When he looked, there was a cake baked on the coal and a cruse of water at his head. Then the angel came a second time and fed him once more and Elijah was able to travel for forty days on this food. It is understood that the Heavenly spirits materialized the food.

Jesus multiplied the loaves and fish to feed four thousand people on one occasion and did the same for five thousand men plus women and children on another occasion. On both of these occasions the food was materialized from the spirit world to where Jesus was.

In the story of the prophet Elisha (II Kings: 4-7) a woman whose husband had died, asked Elisha for help because her husband's creditors were coming to take her two sons for bondsmen. All she had in the house was a pot of oil, so Elisha told her to borrow as many vessels as possible from her neighbors and pour the oil into them. Precious oil was materialized and the woman continued to pour from her pot until all the vessels she had borrowed were filled to the top miraculously. The one pot of oil filled all of the vessels and Elisha told her to go and sell the oil and pay her debt.

On another occasion, a man brought Elisha twenty loaves of barley and some corn and Elisha asked him to give the food to his prophets but the man said, "What, should I set this before an hundred men?" (Kings 4:42-44) But the men were fed and with some left over.

Jean Baptiste Maria Vianey was a Catholic priest who lived in France in the nineteenth century. He maintained a home for poor children and one day discovered that there were no provisions left except a few handfuls of grain in the corn bin. With a heavy heart he made up his mind to send the children away, but before doing so, he offered one more prayer to God for help. On going back to the corn bin he found it filled with grain to the top. All of his parishioners came to see the so-called miracle. The event caused great sensation throughout the entire district. (Published by Gebr). Steffen, Limburg a.d.Lahn)

The first miracle that Jesus performed was to turn water into wine while at the wedding. When his mother told him that they were out of wine, he mentioned that his time had not yet come, because the spirits helping him needed time to transform the water into wine. Since Jesus was highly clairvoyant and could see all that the spirits were doing, he could see that the work had not yet been accomplished. Materialization and de-materialization takes time, it is not instant, only because Jesus could see by clairvoyance when the work was complete could he announce it.

In order for people to see an apparition, they must either be clairvoyant or the spirit must materialize, or a combination of both where a person might be partially clairvoyant, which means clear sight, and would only require a partially materialized spirit to see that spirit. In order for the spirit to materialize, they must borrow the od or energy of the material world and condense it for this purpose. Depending on the amount of od available, the spirit will materialize part of itself or all of itself. Perhaps only the head will be seen or only the top half of the body, by the choice of those spirits. If enough energy is available, the whole body will be visible, and the appearance would not be any different from any other similar creature. When a complete body cannot be seen, this means that there was just enough energy to materialize only part of it. Depending on the amount of energy made available, the spirit may be of differing sizes. The spirit may appear the height of a child if that is all the od they have at their disposal. With enough od, a spirit can appear to be the size of a standard human.

In the case of a materialization medium, the medium would be the main source of od and can release enough energy to enable one or more spirits to make themselves visible or partly visible to human eyes. Other assistant od sources such as we read about in the temple of Moses with the "tent of testimony" (Num 18) are usually required to enact full materialization. These were the reasons for the many offerings in the Old Testament. Aaron was the high priest. Since this requires more of the od possessed by the medium, his own spirit must be more detached from his body. If the materialization is to be complete enough to allow the spirit to look like a terrestrial being, the medium's od alone is not sufficient, and matter must be taken from his physical substance. For this reason, in materialization of this nature, a medium surrenders a great part of his physical weight which is restored to him in full when the

36

materialization has come to an end. This materialization always takes place in proximity to the medium. Once the spirit dematerializes, the matter belonging to the medium is returned to him. The medium would have lost weight while the materialization was visible.

Carlos Mirabelli was a materialization medium who lived in Sao Paulo, Brazil between 1889 and 1951. He was a universal medium, his odic power was adequate for phenomena embraced by all types of spirit communication. There is a record of his mediumship being observed by at least 557 persons of notable repute. Among his mediumistic occurrences, there were many instances of apparitions of complete humans, some which were recognized by the supervising scholars. Some of his materializations required so much od that part of the substance of his corporeal body was dissolved and used for materializing the spirit. There is a picture of Mirabelli where his forearms are completely dissolved while the apparition could be seen, and another where the apparition took his place at the table with the supervisors and looked like one of them. Unfortunately there was no one to make sure that all of this communication was with God's spirits so there were apparitions of all types, good spirits and low ones, but there was no denying that the apparitions occurred.

In a book by Johannes Greber called "Communication with the Spirit World of God", a very high spirit tells us the following, "The greatest obstacle in the way of seeing the truth is the erroneous conception of the terms 'spirit' and 'matter'. Once the fact is recognized that the nature of the spirit creation is the same as that of material creation, and that they differ only in the manner in which they manifest their existence, most of the difficulties that prevent a proper understanding in the field of spirit communication will disappear of their own accord. You will then recognize that created spirits possess the same organism in spirit form as terrestrial beings possess in material form; that the body has been cast over the shape of the spirit, and that nothing can be contained in the material casing which is not present in the spirit-shape also. And it will be further recognized that the 'beyond' resembles the 'here' in every way, with the sole difference that 'here' all things are matter and that 'there' all things are spirit."

"You are visible to your fellow creatures from the fact that you have a material body. Your material body is only the material shell of your spirit with all of its organs, every organ found in your body has its counterpart in a spiritual state in your spirit.

If a disembodied spirit wants to appear to terrestrial eyes, it must clothe its spirit form and all of the members with a shell of matter, which it produces by means of the condensation of terrestrial od.

Materialization by a full trance medium.

In the case of a spirit so materialized the human eye can discover nothing to distinguish it from an everyday person. The spirit has skin, bones, all external organs, fingernails, hair and teeth, as well as inner organs like a heart which beats, blood which circulates and whatever else is present in any normal flesh and blood human being". You can experience these materializations in some seances.

The medium is in the tent – the apparition
is to the right.

The tent is used to hold the energy or od.

Notice the cord of energy or od between the
medium and the apparition.

Whether the medium is working with high spirits or low spirits, the effect is still the same. The laws are made by God but they are not always necessarily used for His purposes. Everyone lives under the same laws even if they say they do not believe in God, they still use what God has provided. In the case of the evil spirits, those which have severed their relations with God, this power is however circumscribed within very definite limits, whereas it can be put to use by God's spirits to an unrestricted extent since God is the exhaust-less source of power.

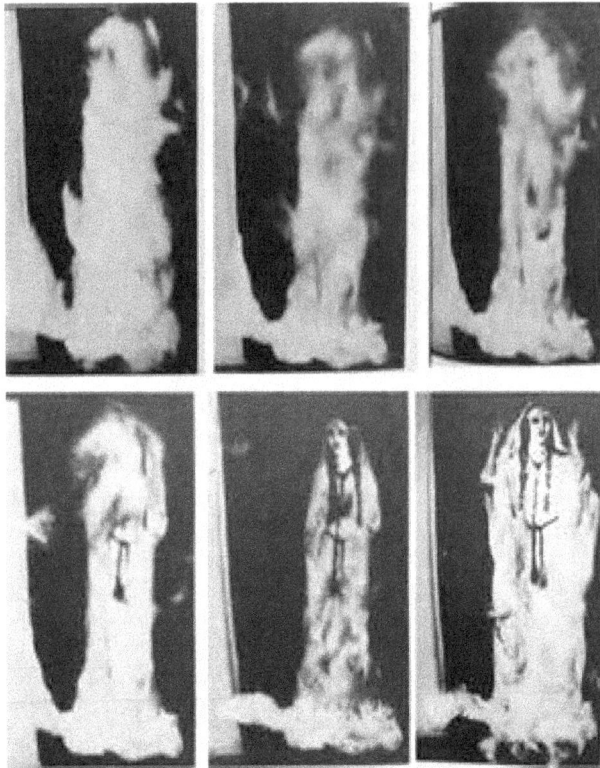

The process of materialization

You can now understand how Adam was created on the physical plane. Adam was a spirit before God materialized him on this planet. God used the energy of the earth to materialize him. The Bible says this in (Ecc. 3:20), "All go to the same place; all come from dust and to dust all return", which means that our physical body is formed from the material of the earth and it returns to the earth when our spirit departs from our physical body after death.

The story in the Book of Genesis in the Bible is very confusing because it tells of Adam & Eve when they lived in the spirit world and then how God created their physical bodies on earth, but these are two different occurrences. Adam and Eve had been created in Heaven along with all other spirits that God had created, which includes all of us. After their disobedience, along with one third of Heaven, including us, God sent them to a lower realm in Heaven, called Paradise, in a place called the Garden of Eden, to give them another opportunity to rethink their choice. After disobeying a second time, by following the path of evil, greed, lust and avarice, God cast them out of the Garden of Eden in Paradise and out of the Heavenly realms altogether into a much lower realm, we call hell. Then God created the physical universe as a means for the fallen spirits to learn to be good once again, to be tested, and pass these tests of good character once again

In the story of the old testament in Genesis where it mentions Eve materializing from Adam's od, the translation uses the words "Adam's rib". This is not an entirely clear translation, nor understanding of the original meaning of "odic energy" by the translator. Eve was materialized using the energy of Adam who was a medium by reason of having been formed directly from earthly od/energy. His spirit was able to release physical energy to a greater degree than if he had been born. In her case, God used some of the general od from the material body of Adam to materialize Eve.

Since all spirit materializations are of a temporary nature only and since Eve's body needed to be permanent, some of the physical substance had to be taken from Adam. This portion that was not returned to Adam was given back to him by drawing from the od/energy of the earth in the correct amounts of material needed by his body. The writer of this part of the Bible explains this by an analogy, "And God caused a deep sleep to fall upon Adam, and he slept, and He took one of his ribs, and closed up the flesh instead thereof" (Gen 2:21-22). The deep sleep was a mediumistic sleep or a full trance state. Once it is understood that people can de-materialize and materialize, it is easier to see how spirits can reach mankind with that same energy.

In the story of Abraham, three spirits materialized and spent some time with Abraham and Sarah. Abraham had Sarah make cakes for them while he fetched a young calf and had it prepared for the visitors. These spirits were able to eat a meal with them before continuing on their trip. "...and he stood by them under the tree, and they did eat". (Gen 18:2-8).

After his death, Jesus appeared to his apostles while they were fishing, "When they landed they saw a charcoal fire and a fish broiling in it. There was also some bread there" (John 21:9), Jesus was completely materialized and ate with his apostles.

41

Jesus also materialized for his apostles and asked them, "Have you any food here? They gave him a piece of broiled fish, and he ate it in their presence". (Luke 24:41)

When John the Baptist was baptizing Jesus, a holy spirit materialized in the shape of a dove and a voice was heard, saying,"Thou art my beloved son, in whom I am well pleased" (Mark 1:11).

Jesus took Peter, James and John to a mountain where he was transfigured and appearing with him, Moses and Elijah who were speaking to him. Then a voice came out of a bright cloud saying, "This is my beloved son, in whom I am well pleased, hear ye him" (Mat 17:1-5). Here is an example of materialization and voice from the cloud.

By these examples, we can see that a completely materialized person is no different from a physical person and can perform all the same tasks as a physical person. Many people have been entertained by materialized Heavenly spirits and were not aware of it, which is not always necessary so long as the lesson is understood by the recipient.

In the Bible, the most well known example of materialization is in the story of Moses. Four hundred years before Moses was alive, Joseph, the son of Jacob, had been sold into Egypt, and later was able to bring all of his family there because of the famine. In time, these Israelites had become a very large population and Pharaoh was concerned that they would join with his enemies and fight against him, so he devised a plan where he would kill all the newborn boys and since the girls could be married into the Egyptian population and be assimilated in this way, the Israelite population could be exterminated.

Moses from birth had been saved by his mother and was, as a foundling, raised by Pharaoh's daughter. In this way he had an opportunity to acquire all manner of education, making him qualified to run a country. But he left Egypt after being discovered protecting his people against Pharaoh, having killed an Egyptian guard who was beating a Hebrew.

God chose Moses to return to Egypt to rescue his people with the aid of his brother, Aaron. When Moses and Aaron confronted Pharaoh to let the Israelite leave, God helped him with many materializations to prove Moses to the people and to prove to the Egyptians that He was sent by God.

The first materialization was to change Moses' rod into a serpent, and the king had his magicians, also called mediums, do the same thing. Then God had Moses use his rod to change all of the waters to blood and Pharaoh's magicians were able to do the same. At Moses' command, God's Heavenly spirits materialized frogs and the magicians were able to compete only up to a certain extent. But when Moses produced lice, the magicians were unable to do the same and they begged Pharaoh to let the people go since they agreed that this was the finger of God. It took several other materializations from God through Moses to convince Pharaoh to free the people: flies, animal disease, boils, hail, locusts, plus three days of darkness. It was not until God took the lives of all the firstborn of Egypt, just like Pharaoh had done to the Israelites, that Pharaoh finally allowed them to leave.

The great battle between Moses, as God's champion against the magicians of Egypt, as Satan's minions, is an example of extraordinary amounts of spiritual phenomena used on both sides of the spirit world, both the angels of Heaven and the evil spirits of hell. God allowed the evil spirit world to try to convince the Hebrews not to follow Moses, while the good spirits, the angels of Heaven, gave plenty of evidence to the Hebrews of their support. In the end, it was God who chose the outcome. God's punishment on Pharaoh, by the death of his own first born son, and the Egyptians was justly given by God, and chosen by Pharaoh himself of what the punishment would be by deciding to kill all the newly born Hebrew boys.

After Moses and the people left Egypt and traveled through the desert, God materialized food for them in the shape of manna, when He "rained bread from Heaven" (Ex 16:4), and water from the rock (Ex 17:6). Also, after the forty years in the desert, the people's clothing were not worn out. The reason they lived in the desert for forty years was to be tested and strengthened against material greed and the Egyptian false religions. In the end, the older generation who could not break their negative habits and continued in their idol worship and were stuck in their old beliefs, had died off. Even now, we have many people who do not understand what they really believe and are not open to understanding, but fight to continue in their traditions, even after the truth is revealed to them.

Another account of materialization of the battle between good and evil is found in the story of the Prophet Elijah against the hundreds of prophets of Baal during the reign of King Ahab and his non-Hebrew wife, Jezebel. The people were split between following God's prophet, Elijah, and following King Ahab's evil prophets of Baal. Then Elijah had Ahab gather his four hundred and fifty prophets of Baal and the four hundred prophets of Jezebel, and Elijah asked the people to follow God or Baal after each had demonstrated their power. He had Baal's prophets make an altar and lay the sacrificial meat on it and light no fire under it, and he did the same. Then he asked the prophets of Baal to pray to Baal to light the wood and burn the sacrifice and Elijah would pray to God to effect the same result. They were to see which one answered the prayer and burn the sacrifice. The god who answered would be from that day the one the Israelite would follow. The prophets of Baal prayed all day and nothing happened, then by evening Elijah told the people to pour water on his sacrifice three times over, and when he prayed to God, a fire came down from Heaven and burned the sacrifice, the wood, the rocks, the dust and even all the water from the trench. This was the deciding factor for the Hebrew nation on which God they would follow.

SPEAKING MEDIUMS

The most beneficial of the mediums for communicating truth are the speaking mediums. The Bible refers to this as prophets speaking in a language that is understood (1st Cor 14). Some are deep trance and others are part trance. The deep trance mediums are those whose spirit can leave their body altogether and another spirit can enter and deliver the message using the medium's organs of speech. A deep trance medium is entirely unconscious of anything spoken through him, while a part trance medium is aware of another spirit speaking through his body. The degree of trance can be understood by the levels of consciousness by the medium who owns the body. Some mediums are entirely aware of what is being said through them, while other part trance mediums might be only aware that something is being communicated through them but not knowledgeable of the information itself. Another form that has been used for trance is, "religious ecstasy". A common term used nowadays is called "channeling".

"There was a difference between the manner in which Moses inquired of God and that in which it was done by the people. To the solemn inquiries addressed to God, Moses as the representative of all the people, is answered by Jehovah through the pillar of cloud that rested on the Ark of the Covenant, whereas when individuals inquired of God, their answer came not through the pillar of cloud but through another channel,

44

which although not clearly defined, is sufficiently well indicated to leave no doubt on that score in the mind of anyone familiar with the subject. We learn that Joshua, the servant of Moses was not allowed to leave the Tent, therefore there must have been a reason for his constant presence there. Joshua was specially appointed to act as a medium for those of the people who desired to inquire of God concerning their private affairs. It is expressly stated that every one who sought Jehovah went out into the tent of meeting. No fixed hours for 'inquiring of God' having been set, Joshua was obliged to be present in the Tent at all times so that he might be available to all as a medium for transmitting the lord's answers".

DIRECT WRITING MANIFESTATIONS

Direct writing is entirely different from the writing done by mediums, being produced by the spirit itself which makes use of the odic force from the medium or from nature, and does not use the medium's hand. The spirit materializes its own hand to write. The first set of tablets bearing the Ten Commandments were written on Mount Sinai by the hand of God as related in the book of Moses. "And the Lord said unto Moses, Come up to me into the mount, and be there, and I will give thee tables of stone, and a law, and commandments which I have written, that thou mayest teach them (Ex 24:12). When Moses came down from the mountain to share this gift with the Hebrews, he found them having returned to their worship of the Egyptian golden calf, Aaron was ignored. Moses, in anger, threw the tablets at the golden calf, destroying them along with the calf idol. Moses returned to the mountain top a second time to receive a second copy of the ten commandments.

When the Israelites has been taken prisoners by Babylon, King Belshazzar made a great feast to his lords and drank from the sacred vessels which his father had taken from the temple of the Israelites. Suddenly, a hand appeared on the wall of his royal palace and the king saw the palm of the hand as it wrote. " In the same hour came forth fingers of a man's hand, and wrote over against the candlestick upon the plaster of the wall of the king's palace and the king saw the part of the hand that wrote" (Dan 5:5). This was a materialized hand of a messenger angel of Heaven that came to warn King Belshazzar that he was going to die and that God was taking his kingdom from him. Daniel was the only person who could read the writing, and that very night the king was slain and the army of the Medes invaded and took his kingdom

UFO'S

These days there are alternate beliefs growing about the meaning of the final war between good and evil. Some groups of people are expecting the end times to be brought about by aliens from another planet. Although there are many forms of life on many planets, there is no reason to believe that a planet near to us would send people here to destroy us, and there has never been a time when anyone from another planet has ever visited earth. The meaning of the end time struggle for the hearts of the people of earth between Heaven and hell that is described in the Book of Revelations, has been slowly altered by some groups to no longer describe a spiritual battle, but a type of Hollywood version of alien invasion from another planet. This deception, similar to the deceiving prophets of Baal, is meant to keep the minds of people busy in nonsensical theories long enough so that they miss the opportunity in this life to change their bad habits, and self-deceived traditions, and to miss the opportunity to learn from the holy spirits of Heaven rather than the false prophets of today.

There definitely are many UFO"s seen by many people but remember that UFO stands for 'unidentified flying object', which tells us that they have not been identified at least during our time. If science has its way of attributing everything to man and nothing to God, then mankind will never know what these objects are. But it is easier for those who have read the Bible and understand that God does have the ability to move in our world whenever He wishes, and so He can send His holy spirits to this planet if He wants to.

In the old testament, there are several accounts of UFO encounters, these were attributed then by the people of that day as manifestations from spirits from Heaven. As we have learned earlier, the angels who appeared to Daniel and others were materialized spirits from Heaven, come to deliver a message from God (Dan 9:21). In (Joel 2:30) it says "I will show wonders in the Heavens and on the earth..." God can allow a mode of transportation for His Heavenly spirits as the need arises. Many people have seen these crafts which look like clouds in the daytime and fire at night.

When Elijah was leaving the earth, he did not die as all other humans. The story tells of a chariot of fire and horses of fire that appeared between him and Elisha, and Elijah was taken up in a whirlwind and Elisha caught Elijah's mantel. Elisha identified the manifestation as coming from Heaven, a materialization that in its power de-materialized Elijah's physical body, and took his spirit to Heaven. This might also have been the way Enoch was taken by God at the end of his physical life (Gen 45:23-24)

POSITIVE AND NEGATIVE ENERGY

People often talk to their plants and that has been understood to help them thrive whereas there are some who believe this has no benefit. There have been some experiments done that show how water changes its crystals when different words are spoken to them, and also that different types of music has an effect on water.

Dr. Masaru Emoto from Japan, born in Yokohama in 1943, a doctor of alternative medicine, was introduced to the concept of micro cluster water in the United States, and Magnetic Resonance Analysis technology. His quest began to discover the mystery of water. He realized that it was in the frozen crystals that water showed its true nature. There is one basic truth we all learn early, positive, compassionate words comfort and heal; negative words and insults hurt. Until recently we knew this only because we could feel it, now we can actually see it. Thanks to the experimental work of Dr. Masaru Emoto, we can look at water, and its frozen crystals, to confirm the healing power of beautiful music, positive thinking, uplifting speech and prayer.

By exposing water to a particular word or piece of music, freezing it and photographing the ice crystals formed, Dr. Emoto has shown that from beautiful words and music, come beautiful crystals, and from mean-spirited, negative words come malformed and misshapen crystals. When we remember that the adult human body is approximately 70% water and infant bodies are about 90% water and that the earth is mostly water, we can believe that we can affect the vibration of people by our words etc

.

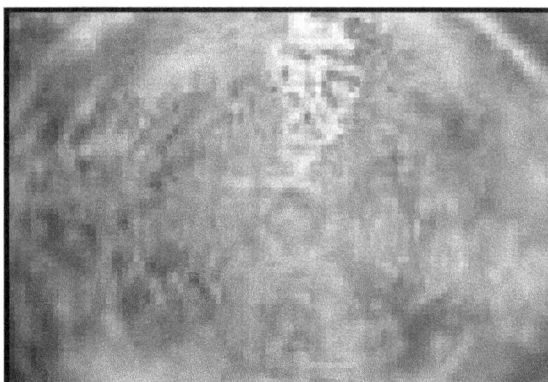

A heavy metal song

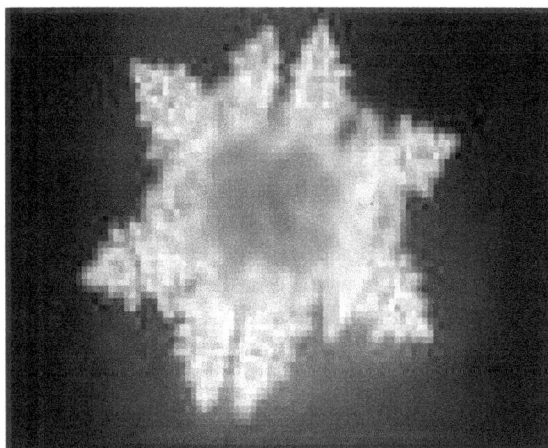

Amazing Grace

48

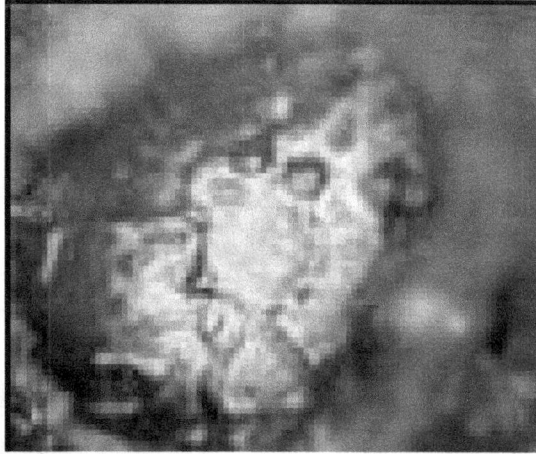
Before prayer

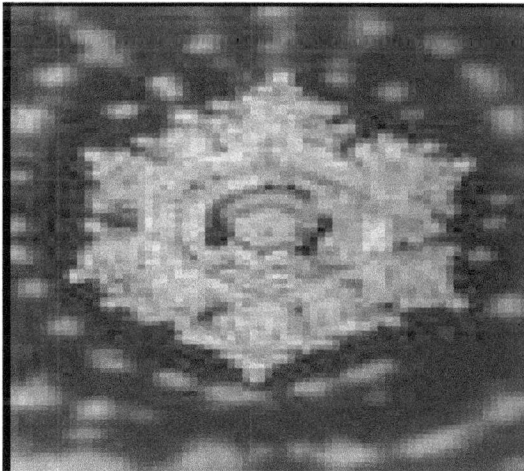
After Prayer

49

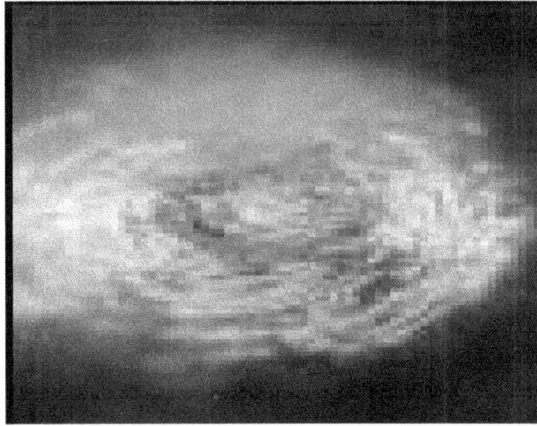
Your Fool (words)

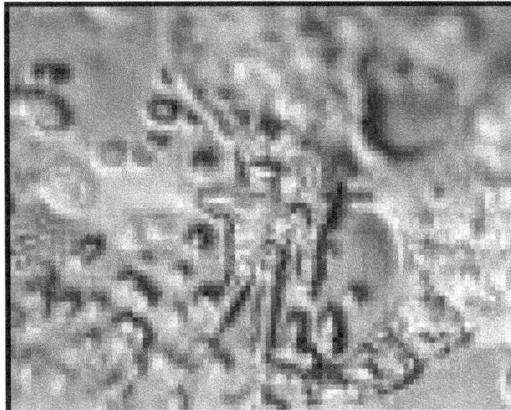
You disgust me (words

Truth (words)

Thank you (words)

Dr. Emoto also performed another experiment with rice. He placed rice in two jars and covered them with water. Every day for one month he had children speak over the rice. Over the first jar they said, "you fool", and over the second jar, they said, "thank you". After one month, the rice in the first jar had turned black while the rice in the second jar had fermented and gave off a pleasant aroma. Others have performed this same experiment with imilar results.

You fool   Thank you

After David had slain the giant, King Saul brought him into his court. Because David knew how to fight wars, the people praised him and this made King Saul very jealous and he would go into terrible fits and tried to kill David. The Bible says that the spirit of God departed from Saul and an evil spirit was upon Saul. The only way that Saul could get out of his evil fits was to have David play his harp and sing hymns. From this we can deduce that harmonious music can raise people's vibration and remove low spirits.

On this realm, we are surrounded by spirits. There are many good spirits sent to us by God whose purpose is to assist us in all of our spiritual and physical endeavors. Without their help, we would never on our own, manage to even stay alive. We are all given a special angel at birth as a guardian spirit and they remain with us throughout our lives. Mothers, although they might be careful to watch over their children, have to admit that there must be someone looking after them when they see the precarious situations their children have been placed in, and the times that their children might have been protected or helped by unseen forces.

Like King Saul, if we are evil minded or careless, we attract low and evil spirits and our life is not as peaceful as it should be. But if we follow a more harmonious path and are watchful of our thoughts and actions, we have more of God's spirits as fellow travelers. The spirits with Saul were so evil that all they wanted to do was to kill David, and it makes us wonder how murderers have come to the point of all this evil if not by the obsessions or possessions of evil spirits.

It is very beneficial to monitor one's thoughts before they become actions. We can help ourselves by avoiding movies and music that elevates evil to appear as good or as acceptable behavior. If our desires are not any that we could attribute to assistance from God, it behooves us to check our thoughts and to recognize the outcome if an action is followed through.

The people who incarnate on earth make up the embodiment of spirits who rebelled in Heaven along with Adam and Eve when they sided with Lucifer against Christ, and now are materialized on this realm in an effort to relearn how to be good and harmonious once again. This is why we must make a conscious decision in this life to abandon evil and selfish desires and to follow the teachings of Christ. It is not an easy task for many with Lucifer and his forces having such a strong influence in our daily lives.

CLAIRVOYANCE AND CLAIRAUDIENCE

Those who are clairvoyant or clairaudient are not to be included among mediums. They do have mediumistic powers but are not true mediums. With them it is their own spirit which is active, which sees and hears, whereas in mediums properly so called, it is a strange spirit which acts while the medium's spirit is temporarily dispossessed. Although they can see or hear they are not an instrument of these spirits, but their spirit can detach itself from the body to a greater or lesser degree. A spirit so detached and partly withdrawn from the body thereby becomes independent of the latter's physical senses, and assumes the faculties and properties of a discarnate spirit, seeing, hearing and feeling into the spirit world. The sensory powers of the person depends on the extent to which it is detached and according to the purity of the od surrounding it just as the purity attributed to the quality of glass.

There are many references to clairvoyance and clairaudience in both the Old and New Testaments. When the angel of the Lord smote the people of Israel with the pestilence as a punishment, "David saw the angel who was striking down the people", (2nd Samuel 24:16)

Jesus, when he was on earth tells the people that they will see the heavens open and the messengers of God descending and ascending above him. So Jesus was both clairvoyant and clairaudient. It was by this means that God's holy spirits showed Jesus which of the men could be chosen by God to be his apostles, he didn't just decide when he saw them..

When Jesus saw Nathaniel coming towards him he said, "Here is an Israelite such as he ought to be, a man in whom there is no flaw". Nathaniel asked, "How do you know me?" and Jesus said, "I saw you before Philip called you, sitting under the fig tree". Jesus had seen Nathaniel by clairvoyance before Nathaniel even knew that he was coming.

Jesus going through the town of Sychar in Samaria, stopped to rest and asked the Samaritan woman for water. At that time, the Jews and the Samaritans were not on good terms so she was surprised that he asked her for water. During the conversation, Jesus saw her life by clairvoyance and she ran to tell her people that Jesus had told her all about herself, so could he be the Messiah? The village people invited him to stay with them which he did for two days teaching them with the result that many were converted.

Elisha foresaw the destiny of Hazael by a clairvoyant vision given to him by holy spirits. He saw the cruelties Hazael would practice on the Israelites, because he had been allowed to see how he would rule the country, "Jehovah has let me see your reigning over Aram" (2nd Kings 8:11).

Daniel saw and heard the spirit of Gabriel who came to answer his prayer. Those who were with Daniel fled because they felt the spirit although they could not see or hear him. Daniel fell to the ground from weakness, because the spirit had materialized with the aid of Daniel's odic energy.

Jeremiah was one of God's prophets and was given many messages from the spirit world to warn the people of the disasters to come if they did not obey God. The Bible does not say in what form Jeremiah received the messages and visions but we can assume that he was clairvoyant and clairaudient, though he may well have also been a deep trance medium because his assistant, Baruch, followed him everywhere and wrote down the messages that were given to Jeremiah.

All the stories of the apostles receiving help was through clairvoyance and clairaudience. The angel who appeared to Peter in (Acts 12:7) and told him to get dressed and he let him out of prison. Paul, by clairvoyance also saw the angel who appeared to him and also let him out of prison. All of the healing by the apostles were with the aid of God's spirits. The apostles did not choose leaders unless told by the holy spirits, and they did not go to preach wherever they wanted nor did they preach whatever they wished. Paul was not one of the original apostles, he didn't go to the apostles to learn what Jesus had said. It was a vision and voice by clairvoyance and clairaudience that Jesus revealed himself to Saul, who later changed his name to Paul.

On his trip to Damascus a spirit appeared to Paul and asked him whom he was persecuting and said, "I am Jesus of Nazareth whom you are persecuting", Paul became temporarily blind by the light of the vision, and his friends scattered from fear although they did not see or hear Jesus.

On his voyage to Italy, Paul told the crew to take courage and eat, that they would not die in the storm, "For last night an angel of the God I belong to and serve stood before me..."(Acts 27:21) and said, "Courage! As you have testified for me at Jerusalem, so you must testify at Rome" (Acts 23:11).

When Paul had come to Troas, there appeared suddenly in the night a man of Macedonia who besought Pau, "Come over to Macedonia and help us" (Acts16:9).

Mary, the mother of Jesus, saw the angel Gabriel who told her that she was to be the mother of Jesus, who would be a son of God. He also told her that her cousin Elizabeth was also going to have a son, and that was John the Baptist.

Joseph was told, "Arise, take the child and his mother and flee to Egypt", (Mat 2:13) and later he was told to go to the land of Israel, to Nazareth because the danger was over.

VISIONS and MESSAGES

Visions are also given to us by the use of energy or od, provided by either the person for whom the vision is meant or by the od available near the person.

The Book of Revelations is an account of visions given to John of all the occurrences in the latter days on our physical earth. We have had a great deal of difficulty understanding the visions, partly because they speak of many things in the future that were not yet invented, such as our means of communication and the arsenal that would be used to destroy parts of the earth. John described his visions using descriptions of things he had seen in his lifetime; for instance, he had never seen a helicopter and pictured it using words that describe an insect with human attributes. There are a few who now are able to decipher some of the revelations at this time, since we are living near the end of the age. In (Daniel 12:4) Daniel is given this message: "But thou, O Daniel, shut up the words, and seal the book, even to the time of the end".

King Nebuchadnezzar of Babylon was given a vision showing him the future. It showed a man with a head of gold, a chest and arms of silver, belly and thighs of brass, legs of iron and feet of iron and clay. Daniel interpreted the dream to foretell the next kingdoms to come after King Nebuchadnezzar, who was the head of gold. All of them would come to an end with God replacing the last one with His own kingdom at the end of this era.

Daniel himself had a great vision which corresponds with the vision of John in the book of revelations, which is the last book in the Bible. It was a vision depicting the four beasts representing the four kingdoms of the earth. Some who study the book of revelations compare Daniel's vision to that of John the revelator in order to explain the future of this earth towards the end of this era.

Jacob while on his way to Haran to meet his new wife had a vision, "He dreamed and behold a ladder set upon the earth, and the top of it reached to Heaven, and behold the angels of God ascending and descending on it". (Gen 28:12)

Jesus was the greatest of all developed mediums, because he is the greatest of all spirits created by God, and gifted with the greatest purity and greatest power of all under God, he often spoke of the Kingdom of Heaven and encouraged people to seek this Kingdom. In the Lord's prayer we say, "Thy Kingdom come". The kingdom of God is filled with the pure spirits of Heaven, whose interest is to observe and guide incarnated creatures on the physical realm, to assist in their progression. The spirits must be tested, as from (1 John 4:1-6), to see if the manifesting spirits are from God. These will affirm that Jesus was the Christ who came from Heaven and defeated Lucifer, other lesser spirits will not admit this.

WASHINGTON'S VISION

In more recent times, George Washington who was a man of prayer, had a vision. He went to the thicket many times to pray during the winter his army was at Valley Forge. At that time he was given a vision and a prophecy. The account of this vision was given in 1859 by an old soldier who gave it to a writer, Wesley Bradshaw, who published it. In the vision God revealed to George Washington that three great perils would come upon the republic.

He was sitting at a table engaged in preparing a dispatch and as he looked up he saw a beautiful being. He was unable to move or speak and felt as if paralyzed which tells us that the spirit was using his energy. Then he heard a voice say, "Son of the Republic look and learn". He saw a dark shadowy being moving from Europe to America. He was told that America was going through the first peril at that time which was the war to secede from Great Britain.

Then he saw villages, towns and cities spring up until the whole land from the Atlantic to the Pacific was dotted with them.

57

A second time, the angel said, 'Son of the Republic, look and learn", and he saw the inhabitants of America setting themselves against each other, but then a bright angel appeared with the word "Union" traced on its brow. He placed a flag between the divided nation and said, "Remember, ye are brethren". Instantly the inhabitants, cast down their weapons and united around the National Standard. This was a vision of the Civil War.

Then a third time the voice said, "Son of the Republic, look and learn", and the angel blew three distinct blasts on a trumpet and he saw a great battle that involved the nations of Europe, Asia and Africa, and from these continents arose thick black clouds that were soon joined into one and they marched by land and sailed by sea to America which was enveloped in the volume of the cloud. Then the cloud receded and the angel who bore the word "Union", appeared holding the American flag in one hand and a sword in the other, it descended from Heaven with a legion of white spirits. And the angel cried with a loud voice, "While the stars remain, and the heavens send down dew upon the earth, so long shall the union last".

When this was over, the angel who had first appeared said, "Son of the Republic, what you have seen is thus interpreted. Three great perils will come upon the Republic. The most fearful for her is the third, but the whole world united shall not prevail against her. Let every child of the Republic learn to live for his God, his land and Union". George Washington felt that he had seen the birth, progress and destiny of the United States.

MEDIUMS OF OUR TIME

We have also heard of messages from such people as Nostradamus who wrote his messages in quatrains, using coded phrases in order to prevent persecution. These type of prophecies have been applied time and again to various events, some which prove much accuracy. Edgar Casey also received messages for the future but was better known for helping people in the cures of diseases. Mother Shipman is another well known prophet or medium, who predicted that women would cut their hair short and wear men's clothes. She also predicted that women would care for cats and dogs in lieu of babies, I think we are arriving at this last phase now.

THE FALL OF THE ANGELS

The ruler of this earth realm is Lucifer, he is the one whom we have subjected ourselves to when we chose him for our leader when we fell with Adam and Eve out of Heaven, and a second time when we fell from The Garden of Eden in the spirit realm of Paradise. Most religions teach that we are guilty of 'original sin' all because we are the descendants of Adam and Eve. This does not make any sense, why would God punish us for their sin, after all, we on earth are not punished by the courts for the sins of our parents.

One third of the spirits of Heaven fell with Lucifer when he led the rebellion against Jesus, and since it is the first sin committed after our creation, it is called 'original sin'. We are that one third who fell with Lucifer and are incarnated with this sin. This sin separated us from God and from Heaven.

While there is no verse in the Bible that says a "third of the angels fell from Heaven," some verses, when put together, lead us to that conclusion. Sometime after their creation, and most certainly after the sixth day when everything was declared "very good" (Genesis 1-31), Satan rebelled and was cast out of heaven. "How you have fallen from Heaven, O morning star, son of the dawn! You have been cast down to the earth, you who once laid low the nations!" (Isaiah 14:12). When Lucifer sinned, Jesus said, "I saw Satan fall like lightening from Heaven" (Luke 10:18), and in the book of Revelation, Satan is seen as "a star that had fallen from the sky to the earth" (Rev 9:1).

We are also told that one third of an "innumerable company of angels" (Hebrew 12:32 chose to rebel with him, John saw this great wonder in Heaven, "..an enormous red dragon.. His tail swept a third of the stars out of the sky and flung them to the earth.... the great dragon was hurled down ---- that ancient serpent called the devil, or Satan, who leads the whole world astray. He was hurled to the earth, and his angels with him" (Revelation 1: 3-9).

Since Satan is referred to as a star which fell or was cast down to earth, and Rev 12:4 says a third of the stars were cast out with him, then the conclusion is that the stars in Rev 12 refer to fallen angels, fully one third of the heavenly host. If the one-third number is in fact accurate, then two thirds of the angels are still on God's side, and are still in heaven.

Those of us who had only been followers and not instigators were sent to a spiritual location called the Garden of Eden or Paradise with our leader, Adam, who was a high prince in Heaven. This Garden of Eden in Paradise is still in existence but is not on the material earth, the physical universe had not yet been created. Jesus told the repentant criminal who was crucified beside him, "This day you shall be in Paradise with me", so he was not bringing him to a physical location but a spiritual one.

The story in the Bible, there is no record of them being in Heaven and falling from there to the Garden of Eden, the story is told as one and therefore impossible to understand. In Paradise, God gave these spirits a new opportunity to choose Jesus over Lucifer but they did not change their attitude from rebellious behavior and fell from Paradise to a realm that was almost as low as Lucifer's.

We are not told the nature of the sin, but the Bible uses a metaphor calling it the fruit of a particular tree. The story of the apple is just an analogy and the rest of the story regarding Adam and Eve is also. This might be examined as a more correct interpretation rather than the description of an apple that Eve took a bite of, which God had forbidden. To repeat a crime is to return to the same habit of rebellion which caused the trouble. If harmony, and the fruit of that behavior is life, then continual rebellion is spiritual death. As the Bible records that

God said, "The day you eat of that fruit (of rebellion) you will surely die", (separate yourself from harmony and spiritual life). A similar metaphor is used by Jesus in (John 15:5) when he says, "I am the vine, you are the branches..." That the account of this event is no longer clear in the Bible translations today, critics make it the butt of jokes. Nothing discredits anything more easily than to make fun of it.

Jesus descended into hell after his crucifixion to release us from Lucifer's hold. Christ's victory over Lucifer was the final requirement in this great battle. Many Christian churches teach that Jesus died for all the sins that we have ever committed and for all the sins we will commit in the future, but this is not entirely accurate and not very clear. Even if Jesus died for our sins, that belief alone will not save us, we must still live a life worthy of our re-entry into Heaven. Jesus won this battle and the terms of the treaty were that from that time, Lucifer could no longer hold anyone against their will and that's what is meant in the statement, "the gates of Heaven were re-opened".

Until Jesus died on the cross and descended into hell to win a battle against Lucifer, no one who died a physical death, could enter even the lowest realm of Heaven, which is Paradise, but had to wait in spirit form on this realm. Only those who had been born on earth and had come directly from the realm of Heaven could return home to Heaven, people like Mary, Abraham, Isaac, Jacob, Jeremiah and the other great prophets. This is the meaning of the phrase "born from above". These spirits had not participated in the great rebellion with Lucifer and had not fallen from Heaven, consequently, when they incarnated on earth, they came from Heaven, and also returned to Heaven at the end of their physical life. King David tells us that we was born from below much as all of us are. Once we progress to one of the heavenly realms, we may be able to reincarnate on earth to help others, and since we will have been born from above, we would be able to return to that higher realm, as we would already have earned our salvation.

After this second fall, God with the help of Jesus, created the physical universe to help us work our way through our disobedience in order to return to Heaven. By incarnating over and over again on this planet, we have progressed from the lowest earth form to the human stage. We also can progress in the spirit world while waiting for our next incarnation, and eventually we can stop coming to earth and keep progressing in the spirit world. This earth realm is the highest realm of hell, so we can, from this realm, look forward to returning to Paradise or to a higher realm and work from there. There is also a possibility that, if we have not progressed, we could remain on this earth realm in spirit form, or go to an even lower realm, waiting for a new incarnation.

The word reincarnation often suggests to people, the Hindu explanation of reincarnation where we may come back as an animal, but that is not possible. Even if we have not progressed much in a single life, we cannot move to a lower form because we have progressed from that form. It would be impossible to match the spirit vibrations of a human level spirit with that of an animal or a plant for incarnation.

God is love and would never leave any of His children in hell forever. The belief of an everlasting hell is a man made belief. In the Bible, there is a mistranslation of the word which described the time that would be spent by rebellious humans and spirits. Where the Bible today describes hell as "eternal", used to say "eon" which means an entirely different thing. 'Eon' refers to an elastic period to time, but never can it mean a permanently fixed period lasting forever. It is a wonder why so many Christians take such joy in warning us of everlasting hell and still repeat that it is proof that God is love! This belief causes many to abandon the churches and refuse to believe in God. It is a great sin of the churches today.

The tests of life are meant to refine our spirit and prepare us to live in a higher realm after this life. By placing us in challenging environments, our true character is exposed to us, allowing each person a chance to correct those flaws which hold us back in our ascent to greater realms after this life. If hell were everlasting then none of us would have been able to progress to the human stage on this earth, and none of us could return to Heaven. If a person doubts that we are still on one of hell's realms, look around this planet with all of its troubles and check out our past history. The devil is lord of this world, as Christ said. Paul said that we wrestle not against flesh and blood but against the powers of the spirit. This describes the evil powers that once fell "to the earth" as the Bible says in revelations (12:9), this must be a vision John had of a previous event long ago because Satan is already in earth, this realm and not just this planet. Christ calls Satan the god of this realm.

When Jesus came to earth, one of the things that he attempted to teach the Israelites, his chosen people, was to resume communicating with God's spirit world as in the past. The people, for the most part, were following the laws given to Moses and many other rules that had been added to that system by men and not by God. They had given up communicating with the good spirits. They were now more obsessed with following the rules, many of which were no longer applicable, and many of which they were misinterpreting. Moses was no longer around to help them understand the rules or the reason for them and they had no way of inquiring of God

Jesus spoke often of spirit communication and gave his disciples the holy spirits on the day of Pentecost so they could be reminded of what he had taught them and to understand the plan of salvation that he had just established. The apostles were mediums and taught others using the messages given to them by the holy spirits just as Jesus had done (John 1:51) .

There was a good reason for the apostles to go and teach the Israelites. Things had changed for them and for all future generations. Jesus had not come to earth just to preach and heal people, but to lead the lost in this realm back to Heaven, and to win their freedom in a decisive battle between himself, the King of Heaven against the Lord of the underworld, Lucifer, and Christ was victorious. Jesus remained loyal to God even through the agony of dying on the cross, as difficult as that was to bear, and as it had been planned before his birth. But after his death, he descended into the lowest parts of hell, something he could not do as a physical being, since Lucifer was in the spirit world. There, a battle ensued for the freedom of everyone who had fallen, much like the battle that was fought in Heaven when the disobedient spirits had been cast from Heaven (John 12:31), (revelations 12:7).

The churches teach that our sins are washed away by the blood of Christ, but that meaning today is not understood. What does it mean? It was original sin that Jesus overcame for us, which is the sin of deserting God and Jesus and siding with Lucifer when we, one third of Heaven, were kicked out of Heaven. Jesus' victory over Lucifer when he descended into the lowest hell and abolished his power over us is the redemption of our sins. The sinful nature found in humans is the evidence of a flawed humankind that is striving to change and to improve their lot. But the ultimate goal of returning to Paradise by spirits fallen to the earth could not have been accomplished before Christ won the rights of these repentant souls to be set free by that victory over Lucifer, the lord of darkness (revelation 1:18).

If the teachers of divinity understood this great event, they could do a better job of helping people understand also. They do not understand the reason that Jesus is such a special person to us, so they make up a story that Jesus must be God, or a part of God, which they call a part of the trinity. So in effect they confuse the person of Jesus, and by making him equal to God, they diminish the person of God. They do not stop to think that God is so great and powerful that He could never have been born in a human body. Even when God was on Mount Sinai, He told Moses that he could not see His face and live. God's vibration and energy is so much higher than ours and that is why we are unable to understand the nature of God. The first commandment to "Have no other gods before me" is violated when Bible teachers try to prove the idea of a three-in-one God of the trinity, even though this term is not found anywhere in the entire Bible. They seek to prove their theory through other scriptures, but cannot show actual direct evidence.

In this present time we are again following the rules but have no way to learn or correct our errors unless we return to spirit communication for the correct guidance. We follow man-made rules and not God or Jesus Christ. Many read the Bible and approve of all the errors, while others don't even try to read the Bible, but instead they believe whatever they are told in church without questioning anything. At this rate our progress from this realm will be slow indeed. Jesus, while on earth had great difficulty moving people out of their traditions in order to teach them anything new. We read that the Pharisees were of that type, and we have our own Pharisees today.

THE PHARISEES

In Mathew 23 New Living Translation, Jesus criticizes the religious leaders as follows:

Then Jesus said to the crowds and to his disciples, "The teachers of religious law and the Pharisees are the official interpreters of the law of Moses. So practice and obey whatever they tell you, but don't follow their example. For they don't practice what they teach. They crush people with unbearable religious demands and never lift a finger to ease the burden".

"Everything they do is for show. On their arms they wear extra wide prayer boxes with Scripture verses inside, and they wear robes with extra long tassels. And they love to sit at the head table at banquets and in the seats of honor in the synagogues. They love to receive respectful greetings as they walk in the marketplaces, and to be called 'Rabbi.'

"Don't let anyone call you 'Rabbi,' for you have only one teacher, and all of you are equal as brothers and sisters. And don't address anyone here on earth as 'Father', for only God in Heaven is your spiritual Father. And don't let anyone call you 'Teacher,' for you have only one teacher, the Messiah. The greatest among you must be a servant. But those who exalt themselves will be humbled, and those who humble themselves will be exalted".

"What sorrow awaits you teachers of religious law and you Pharisees. Hypocrites! For you shut the door of the Kingdom of Heaven in people's faces. You won't go in yourselves, and you don't let others enter either".

"What sorrow awaits you teachers of religious law and you Pharisees. Hypocrites! For you cross land and sea to make one convert, and then you turn that person into twice the child of hell you are"!

"What sorrow awaits you teachers of religious law and you Pharisees. Hypocrites! For you are careful to tithe even the tiniest income from your herb gardens, but you ignore the more important aspects of the law—justice, mercy, and faith. You should tithe, yes, but do not neglect the more important things. Blind guides! You strain your water so you won't accidentally swallow a gnat, but you swallow a camel".

"What sorrow awaits you teachers of religious law and you Pharisees. Hypocrites! For you are so careful to clean the outside of the cup and the dish, but inside you are filthy—full of greed and self-indulgence! You blind Pharisees! First wash the inside of the cup and the dish, and then the outside will become clean, too".

"What sorrow awaits you teachers of religious law and you Pharisees. Hypocrites! For you are like whitewashed tombs— beautiful on the outside but filled on the inside with dead people's bones and all sorts of impurity. Outwardly you look like righteous people, but inwardly your hearts are filled with hypocrisy and lawlessness".

"What sorrow awaits you teachers of religious law and you Pharisees. Hypocrites! For you build tombs for the prophets your ancestors killed, and you decorate the monuments of the godly people your ancestors destroyed. Then you say, 'If we had lived in the days of our ancestors, we would never have joined them in killing the prophets.'

"But in saying that, you testify against yourselves that you are indeed the descendants of those who murdered the prophets. Go ahead and finish what your ancestors started. Snakes! Sons of vipers! How will you escape the judgment of hell?"

(End of bible quote)

FREEDOM TO CHOOSE

Jesus had no patience for the Pharisees who were close minded and were only interested in following the rules of Moses and wouldn't listen to the truths that he was bringing to them.

Our lives are governed, for the most part, by tradition. Different races and different nationalities have different traditions. We could just as easily have been born as a Muslim, a Buddhist, or a Sikh as a Christian. As children, we follow our parent's traditions but only until we reach the age of reason, at which time we need to let go of traditions that only hold us back. Once we have a basis for our lives, traditions can and do become an obstacle toward progress, especially in our spiritual lives. It is our duty to search and to prove all things rather than to rely on everything we are taught. God gave us total freedom to question, to search and to change our beliefs, to work out our own salvation by striving for that which is true. For this reason, God has assigned a guardian angel to each living being so that by guidance, little by little, each one of us might begin to choose the right path to Heaven, over the many will-o-wisps that keep the mind busy on material and worldly minded things throughout our lives. We are not to allow anyone to tell us what to believe, they will not be around to protect us from our errors once we leave this physical life.

Of course, those who think they have an interest in our lives will not be happy, they will perhaps attempt to make us feel guilty for abandoning their traditions, but we must not allow them to hold us back. Even Mary, the mother of Jesus on earth, had to change her idea of what life and salvation was about once Jesus began to teach. She had been raised with the laws of Moses, but it was now time to learn of the new dispensation brought by Jesus. In the time of Moses, a whole generation had to die off before Moses could bring the Israelites to the promised land, because they were unwilling to leave their idol worship and replace it with the belief in 'one God of Heaven'.

The most difficult thing for us to do as humans is to change our thoughts. It is much easier to defend ourselves against change than to alter our thinking. If we were to stop and analyze our thoughts we would recognize that we have not come by most of them through conscious decisions. If challenged, we would have to admit that most of them came to us from someone else, but we do not discard them because it is easier to keep to the status quo even if it makes no sense than to make the effort to re-think our beliefs

If we do not reach our goal in providing a better pattern of thinking for ourselves after we leave this earth, we will have no one to blame but ourselves. There will be no one to listen to our complaints regarding our lack of progress. Traditions are not our best guide on this earthly trip. As it is, we have not yet progressed much past the dark ages physically and spiritually. Leaders today still hold sway over the majority of mankind with superstitions not to be challenged, while others offer a soul-destroying substitute of a life of ease and pleasure.

Today anyone who breaks with tradition in order to study a more productive path other than their religious beliefs, are told that if they believe anything other than what their religious leaders, teachers, and parents interpreted what they think the Bible means, then they are called disloyal, ungodly, heretics, and threatened with a future of eternal hell. So it is with great trepidation that anyone dares to think for themselves.

Communication with spirits is as much a science as any other branch and has its own rules found in nature. Other than speaking to those who have more knowledge of the spirit world, than those in that spirit world, there doesn't seem to be any other way to learn of our destination after our physical death. However, spirit contact is not needed for anyone who has chosen to follow a path of clean living as Christ taught. For other people who are not convinced of an afterlife, they can as individuals, reach their spirit guides of Heaven, following Jesus' guidance, "Ask and it will be given to you, seek and you will find, knock and the door will be opened to you" (Mat 7:7). The most important pattern is to tune in, not unlike tuning in to a radio wave, unless we have that actual frequency we can hear nothing. And every now and then we can run up and down the dial searching for an answer, and we will run into a station or two. Inspirational thought can be advanced by concentration, the more sensitive we become, the less willing we are to run our thoughts sideways instead of upward, the more easy it is. Following good thoughts and making good and clear thinking decisions makes it easier to pull away from worldly thoughts now and then to muse upon higher things.

Mankind always makes errors but why we don't want to learn from them is a mystery. God's angels cannot reach those whose minds are made up already, and who are not curious to find out if what Christ said is really true. If a person decides ahead of time that there is no God and no help from Heaven, it makes the job more difficult for the Heavenly angels to reach them with good and inspiring guidance. Many would rather spend their lives concentrating on being rich or famous and call all those who believe in God and Christ foolish. As the Bible says, God has chosen those whom the world calls foolish, while those who call themselves wise he leaves to their own devices, and will help them only when they ask for help or guidance, to do anything else would be to force a person beyond their free will, and this God will never do.

Even many churches are not interested in learning from God's spirits. They, of course have nobody who can help them understand more, other than the Heavenly spirits. It is the fear of change, that salvation can be lost, or an ultimate punishment might be handed down from Heaven if a single rule learned has been broken. This type of thinking runs counter to a God of love and mercy. And because God is love and He is merciful, we can be assured that God will not give us stone when we ask for bread (Mat 7:9).

If all of nature is present around us to enjoy, with beautiful crystal clear water, fresh forests and bright warm sun to soften the most hardened nature, and to think only for a moment that a God, a creator of love has done this for us when we did not yet ask, what would He do in our personal circumstances to help us understand and to rise above our lower thinking if we call upon him and ask for knowledge, strive for the gifts of

68

wisdom already given to us and create an environment of harmony wherever we live, who can know the future blessings of any person!

It is difficult to convince anyone that their belief is incorrect by just telling them so. The stronger the belief, the more they will defend it, sometimes going through great explanations of why they are correct or by repeating the same learned traditions from childhood over and over.

The people of Jesus' day only knew the Law of Moses. God gave it to them to start them off in a positive direction, but after so many centuries of hearing the laws, they were reluctant to change their thinking and to move on. Jesus wanted them to return to depending on God's holy spirits for further understanding and proved to them that anything was possible with that power. He demonstrated the power of God through the countless miracles, like turning water to wine, multiplying the loaves and fish and by healing their bodies. He had come to heal their spirits and show them the way to Heaven.

For this reason Jesus is called the savior, and indeed he is. Calling upon Christ does not take up his time, for his very existence as Lord over all of God's creation is meant as a guide and help to all of us. The fact that Christ was able to fit himself into a small human body is quite a feat and almost unfathomable, considering that he is also the single spirit whom God appointed over all mankind and all creation, to protect and offer help and guidance to all God's creatures according to their needs. Like a child who asks their father for help might receive a helping hand from an older sibling at the request of the parent, so Jesus is sent to us to help us every day. His angelic helpers are ever available when we call them for truth and guidance and help.

If anyone decides to attempt to communicate with God's holy spirits, here is a rule by which a person can distinguish between the spirits, as the Bible says in (John 4:6). No spirit from God who speaks will call Jesus accursed, and no spirit can speak of Jesus as his Lord unless he belongs to the holy spirits. To ask a spirit to affirm that Jesus of Nazareth was the incarnate Christ, and did defeat Satan for the release of the fallen spirits, is the only way to know the level of spirit being contacted, other than the obvious nature of harmony and intellect which would be found in a higher spirit. Low spirits will not subject themselves to being examined, whereas a spirit from God expects us to ask him where his allegiance lies and whom he follows.

HERE ARE SOME SAMPLES OF MESSAGES FROM HOLY SPIRIT COMMUNICATION DURING PRAYER MEETINGS.

February 5, 1970

There is a realm the beauty of which makes glad the City of God, wherein dwell the Sons of the Most High. Within sight of the light that emanates therein, you once dwelt.

You are now on an evolutionary progress toward that realm. You mortals are on the threshold of once more sitting face to face with Almighty God. This life you lead is but a fragment of eternity, wherein joy abounds and beauty stirs the soul. One's main objective in this life is to grow inwardly with a capacity to love and to banish all inharmonious defects from within your personalities.

It should be with great care that you nurture your spirit with spiritual food, and enhance your mind with great intellectual truths, and expand your consciousness beyond the meager selfish world in which you dwell, to increase your environment and from time to time remove yourselves from the forest that you may see the trees.

You are being drawn together and toward the source of all life with the irresistible love and understanding of the great Father. Further, it is His will that every soul be restored to Him and that none shall be lost.

Avail yourselves therefore to a singleness of purpose, serving but one Master. Do not store up treasures on earth where moth and rust consume, but rather, be exceedingly careful in preparing for that life which is to come, that you be found not lacking in any area.

As you stand on the threshold of this new life, so too, your world is at a threshold wherein the evil forces desire to overtake and enslave the world at large. It is of most importance that you and others like you maintain this vigil, that your nation shall be preserved. If men of your nation and your leaders do not change their ways and return to the faith of their forefathers, we will not be allowed to protect your nation any more than we have been able to protect Jerusalem.

As the spiritual signs appear in your skies once more, take note. The time draws nigh, for there are yet many issues yet to be resolved between Heaven and Hell. There are many principalities and powers still struggling for the upper hand.

We desire that you be our feet and our hands, that we may manifest to the world, displaying the great power that is of God, for there can be no greater mission. There can be no greater work than to serve your fellowman in the highest way.

Go therefore with God. Protect each other with love and remember, most of all, that which affects any one of you, affects all, for you are closely bound with invisible lines of force through which all feeling and sensation transmits. Therefore it is not uncommon, though apart, for you to feel of the distress or happiness of others within your group.

In parting, let us keep our banners high that the victory won by the Christ may not suffer loss but fight for the truth at every turn and great shall be your joy and reward. God undergird you and be with you till we meet again. Thank you and goodnight.

October 31, 1957

Good Evening. May each and every one of you thirst and hunger after righteousness in your search for truth, for the meaning of righteousness is right wisdom, that wisdom which is eternal, whose only source is the omnipotent being that we call God.

Tonight, if but for a brief period due to conditions, I would like to attempt to bring you closer to an understanding of the relationships between the human and the spiritual. First of all, there must be a just cause for the creation of the physical universe if that which is reality, that which is eternally spiritual, was perfect in the beginning. And indeed there is a just cause. This is the main link in the plan to restore the fallen spirits, those who were cast out of Heaven eons of time ago to restore them to their former glory in Heaven.

First of all let us examine the status of those spirits. When they found the revolt which they supported had failed, and because of this open tyranny against God and His Laws, and because of their defection, they tainted their spirits and clouded it with impurities. They found themselves separated from God, and their attitude was chiefly that of arrogance. And as you know, arrogance, when humbled, when forced, becomes sullen and spiteful, and indeed there is no victory in humbling arrogance. In order to restore these fallen spirits to their rightful minds and places, their attitudes must be first corrected.

These spheres of progress in the terrestrial stages were designed just for this purpose, and out of His mercy, these spirits must choose on their own accord, according to their own free will, to take these stages. This well-disposed factor, their conditions of spirit, must take these stages, these life experiences as the road back to God, and all they do must be the exercises of free will, so that the end result would lie in a knowing that is based on experience. These lives of conditioning were further designed that the well within each that is to house the love out of which love flows, must be dug first with its sorrow, the grief and travail that have confronted mankind from all sides. It is a true statement that one can not really feel love for anyone, and that the depth of their love is measured only by the sorrow that has dug this well.

To continue; Out of His mercy, all past experiences of the individual's incarnations are blotted out temporarily as are memories of this arrogance, of these attitudes against their God without prejudice of personalities. You are living in a so-called state of amnesia in which all past habits are but tendencies in your personalities, and these imperfections must be fought on all sides by the individual to increase a more harmonious attitude, and a more loving attitude.

It would drive most mortals mad if they were confronted with their past life experiences. It is more important to anticipate and to prepare for that which is to come, to evaluate the present status only as far as its value and preparation for the life to come. All else that you do here is insignificant and contributes very little to the growth of your spirit. And as your attitudes toward God and your fellow man, and truths change and become altered, then and only then do your spiritual eyes become open, and with a hunger, a new appetite, to find that which was once lost, becomes inflamed with an eagerness to forsake all things, to sell your treasure so to speak, to buy the field that has the greater treasure, this is what was meant by that parable. But if you notice in the parable, you find the treasure of Heaven first before you discard that which you have, for where your heart lies there you will be.

Thank you for listening, and may we in some way answer the eternal questions that confront mankind on all sides, and restore a channel through which truth once more can be available to mankind, through the promises of our Lord and Savior Jesus Christ, who had promised to send the spirits of truth to guide us to all things good.

May this be each individual's goal, to seek God. Because of the worldly idols to keep mankind away from the truth, that occupies their thoughts and time, to such a dangerous degree and pitch, that all thoughts of God are but obscure from their minds, that this need of a thorough going understanding of spirit communication be once more restored to the faithful.

The material must serve man and not the other way around. Once the mind is convinced of the power that answers from above, the problems of the world will be reversed and solutions to mankind's problems will be a simple to reach as waking up in the morning – it will be an automatic reflex. Keep peace as you go.

March 5, 1967

Good Evening. We bring greetings from on high. It may seem incredible to you that there are mighty forces in your atmosphere that are observing the objectives of men. Over the centuries we have observed the material, social and spiritual evolution of your planet. We have also observed the inability of man to live with man and among the most serious causes of the conflict between them is the stubborn resistance to change. Man stubbornly clings to the traditions of the past, steeped in prejudice and error. The great social revolution that is taking place in your planet is to break down the barriers of language, of race and environment. Wherever there is change in these areas of thought, the resistance to this change must be met with revolt and where one school of thought looked upon revolt as insolence and evil, those who support the revolt are considered heroes by their own as regards the birth of your own nation.

The overall picture, the entire purpose, in social and physical evolution is to bring man, that is a cross-section of man, into a point where the general comprehension of the higher proofs can be had and this generation before you in their attempts to be unlike the generation preceding them, are striving for change whereby they will not be acquainted to the old and in so doing they achieve greater freedom to pursue fewer inhibitions to seek out for their heaven with a very healthy curiosity. However, accompanying this great freedom lies the responsibilities and the consequence of the acts of this freedom, the preservation of the principles upon which these freedoms are based must be jealously guarded lest they become obscure and trampled under foot. For these same freedoms that you enjoy must of necessity be guaranteed to all. The foundation of the Kingdom of Heaven is based upon these truths and principles. How else could so large a number exist in perfect harmony and no one shall enter into that kingdom unless so endowed.

Very often, there is demonstrated in the history of past nations, the great freedom available to the individual of this nation, shall indeed be used against him or bring about his destruction. Our concern for your planet is to bring forth a prophet with a new voice that shall inspire and cause direction that we may assist those who await the coming of the Lord. Those sightings that have been viewed in your atmosphere will be called incidental by comparison to that which will transpire. Since all creation is designed for growth and expansion and improvement, time and events have caused our planet to come to a threshold. The door must be opened to a greater understanding that those who will enter may cross the threshold and that you all prepare for the great undertaking of serving God. There shall arise a voice and the power both within and without and many signs in the sky shall call forth from all points of your globe. There is one coming who will bear the mighty truths of the salvation whereby all mysteries shall depart in the light of understanding that these great mighty truths can be spoken, heard and understood.

Gird yourself anew in the element of understanding of faith of that which is to transpire and do not involve yourselves so much with worldly things and free yourselves of those worldly cares that are a yoke. Avail yourselves of the freedom for only then can your express the joy, the excitement of knowing in whom you believe and whom you serve who is the King of Kings and the Lord of Hosts. May His name ring forevermore as the regent of God Himself – the Lord Christ. God be with you. Goodnight.

June 5, 1969

Once again we greet you from the world of spirit. Conditions as not exactly as we would have them, however, this is to be expected for the ruler of this world is indeed hostile to the attempts of anyone in their attempts to communicate with the Holy Spirit World. This indeed is not accomplished without great effort on the part of the instruments present, all of whom during the past fifteen years showed great consistency to bind themselves to the spirits of Christ, and who indeed are a constant threat to the powers of the abyss. The battle can also be felt on the individual level, between all persons regardless of their stature in life, and will continue through the life of each individual, for there is a constant battle between the powers of good and evil for the soul of each individual.

During the days when Christ was on earth, you can imagine the difficulties He had in attempting to teach his followers the knowledge of the questions that confronted each individual concerning the beyond and the life to come, for indeed the truth in its full grandeur is an intellectual food, fit only for those whose minds have reached their full strength. In most cases the truth has to be disseminated selectively according to the ability of the listener to comprehend. You measure your capacities of intelligence according to the capacity to learn, so too we are concerned with each individual who comes into knowledge of the truth on the level to which they have evolved that we may in turn prepare the spiritual food accordingly.

However in answer to your prayers, we shall not content ourselves of merely apprising you selectively, but rather that full understanding of all the questions relating to the truth, to your life, to the Plan of Salvation by which each individual will have evolved, and to the many life experiences that one must undergo in order to achieve that destiny which is the restoration of each individual's soul.

It must be indeed welcome news to those who seek beyond the orthodox realm of teaching to come to the knowledge that God's wisdom has provided that all shall be saved, either in this age or in that age which is to come; that there is no eternal damnation, no eternal death; that the continuity of life is a planned transition where through each life experience there came the wisdom and the knowledge of the inner stature that purifies our souls, that elevates it upon the removal of all inharmonious defects.

Most of the doctrines that confront mankind today have made the truth as so presented unpalatable, and in most cases they partake of this only when brought to their knees. This is by cunning design that Satan has used on mortals throughout the course of centuries; to alter the truth by degrees until it no longer resembles that which was first presented. His main purpose and plan is to divert as many as he can from achieving that life which is the promise and the heritage of the Christian.

Therefore by supplication alone can one achieve the protection and the healing, and this can only come by acquiring the true knowledge and the true faith which unlocks all the doors and provides you with the keys to these doors. Your prayers for healing have indeed been answered and the manner in which to acquire this power and to use it wisely has been provided.

What God requires of each individual is a positive faith, not blind acceptance, that alone can unleash this power into a usable force for good. As you know, this power to some degree lies inert in most individuals and is of no value of its own until this is released by the ability of the mind and the will to direct its flow. Any doubts, no matter how small, how unsuspecting, can impair its use.

Therefore under gird yourselves with a thorough understanding. Partake of the meal of this spiritual food provided for you and then go forth using your various gifts, for the more they are used the stronger they will become, and greater will be your share of the power that emanates from God. These laws are immutable and it requires great effort on the part of the individual. The fruits thereof are quite rewarding. Praise God.

October 28, 1971

We search over the land to see if there are any who truly seek God wherein lies the wisdom to see if there are any who truly seek the counsel of the most high. For the most part men serve their own aim. They are blind, the blind who are leading the blind. The chaos that confronts mankind is a direct result of these causes, but men to do not seek to the knowledge of the cause of their events. They do not seek, for the causes lie hidden in ages past and being denied the counsel of forces who can determine their destinies and this guide them to events today that will have its effect on centuries yet unborn.

We welcome this great opportunity and join forces with you and with those guides and faithful servants of Christ who assist you. We recommend that you do not cause the disdain or set back their work but rather prepare yourselves, for indeed it is a terrible power that comes from on high and shall not be called forth unless you are so equipped to handle it. Great havoc can be wrought with this same power that can heal and restore to normalcy that which has been destroyed and perverted. Chasing little games and will o wisp can drain great energies so vital to the cause.

We have begun. The enemy shall be all around yet can touch you not unless you fall to your baser inclinations that permit these entries. Let us therefore arm ourselves with the armor of God as soldiers of light. Many souls are crying out to God in great need, not physical, but for that grain of truth that can heal the soul, for that pure light that cleanses the spirit, that great wisdom that uplifts, and that great fire that purifies yet does not consume.

Oh, tarry not, yet wait for the spirit to go before you and if he does not go before you, go ye not. Your lives from this moment on will be a great charge and much will be expected of you. Others by the thousands are marshaling their forces, crying out to alter the events, ready to fight to destroy the enemy of truth and to proclaim from the mountain tops the true wisdom of God.

In closing, some of you will be privileged to join us occasionally, for many are visitors on your globe from time to time to perform certain functions. Consider it an honor of the highest esteem that they may walk among you. Prepare your houses therefore and follow the highest spiritual guide in all that you do, for every act of every day is vital.

We shall remain daily at your beck and call to assist you in all that you do. Abide therefore in only those thoughts and teachings that shall bear fruit among you. Till we meet again, I humbly and respectfully serve you and our Master Christ.

The following excerpt is taken directly from "Communication with the Spirit World of God" by Johannes Greber.

The mysterious plan conceived by God in His wisdom, a plan which was hitherto lain hidden, but which was perfect by God, before time began in order that we might be led back to glory." 1st Corinthians 2 : 6, 7

"**AFTER** the revolt of a great part of the spirit-world, God determined upon a plan for saving the unfortunate beings which had fallen into the Abyss, and for bringing them back into His Kingdom. His clemency would be extended first of all to the less guilty, those countless hosts which had deserted Him when they were subjected to trial in the sphere of Paradise. Only after these had been saved, would their corrupters, Lucifer and his lieutenants, be allowed to return to the house of the Father.

"God is just. Those who had been misled were guilty of weakness only, but those who had led them astray had sinned with premeditation, and since their offenses had been fundamentally different, so too would be their punishment, and so too would be their respective roads of escape from the Abyss.

"God's first step toward salvation was the creation of spheres of progress or amendment, disposed in stages after laws incomprehensible to you and conceivable only to the infinite wisdom of God. In his letter to the Ephesians, Saint Paul hints at these steps by which spirits may ascend out of the darkness toward God, by Whom they were created in order to insure the execution of His decree providing that all would once more be reunited with His Son. At this point the original text of the Bible makes use of the metaphor of the erection of a house with its several stories. If you will apply this metaphor in a spiritual sense you will more easily understand what I am about to tell you of the spheres of amendment for the fallen spirits.

"What you call "Hell" is the lowest stage into which they sank. But even Hell has its spheres of progress through which a spirit may climb upward by a change of heart, until it reaches the lowest of the terrestrial spheres. These begin in the lower forms of animal life and advance through the stages of rocks, plants, herbs, flowers, and the higher beasts, arriving at last at the highest of animals known to you as "man". Such terrestrial spheres exist not on your earth only, but also on the other heavenly bodies. There are, therefore, many stages parallel to those on your earth. Moreover, the terrestrial stages exist not only in material shape as you see them in animals, plants and minerals, but there is also a corresponding spiritual shape. and, in consequence a spiritual animal. plant and mineral kingdom embracing all orders and species of living beings, which in the spirit-kingdom are clothed in odic bodies, the counterparts of the material bodies which you see on earth.

"Spirits, parted from their material bodies by corporeal death. enter into the respective parallel spirit-spheres where they remain until they are reincarnated by rebirth on earth. Spirits which have not progressed are reincarnated in the same stage as often as may be necessary to fit them for reincarnation in a higher one.

"Each stage of advance required a special act of God to permit of the desired physical shaping of the spirits, and to this end He created the odic shapes of pairs of spirits corresponding to the shape in question and endowed with the power to reproduce the body peculiar to that stage. The spirits themselves are incorporated in the bodies thus procreated, according to fixed laws which prevail in the spirit-world.

"You mortals cannot indeed understand "how" these processes came about, any more than you really understand the processes of Nature which go on all around you, although you witness them daily with your own eyes. "Your science concerns itself with the problem of descent, particularly with that of the descent of man from the apes."There is no such thing as physical descent of a higher form from a lower one. Plants do not produce animals, nor do the lower animals produce the higher forms. Every form of life breeds true to kind, although within each species there are many races, the individual belonging to races of the same order being mutually capable of reproduction among each other.

"Man belongs to the order of the apes. He is the highest race of this order, and you are correct in saying that the ape is the lowest stage of humanity and that man is the highest of the apes. Man is, therefore, the highest animal on earth. Nevertheless, he has not descended physically from the ape, in spite of the fact that in point of physical development, the ape most closely resembles him.

"Before the first incarnation of the spirit of man in the human body, that spirit inhabited the body of an animal, and is therefore the same spirit rising through the different stages of Nature in constantly increasing perfection.

"These stages undergo no physical changes. They are the same today that they were millenniums ago, even if, in the course of the ages, certain orders died out because spirits were no longer incarnated in them. For this reason God created other and higher forms incarnating in them those spirits which had previously inhabited the extinct species, which had served as intermediate stages in the evolution upward. When they disappeared and the higher forms took their places, the spirits in question were compelled to wait until the replacement had been effected.

"So it is that you find to this day the remains of extinct species of plants and animals that lived in former ages.

"There is no retrogression of the spirit from one stage of progress to a lower one even though a spirit may remain at the same stage for a long time. As I have already told you, a spirit which, when its body dies, has not progressed during its incarnation, must be reincarnated again and again until it is fit to enter the next higher stage. That is true of man also; if, during his life on earth he has made no advance on the road leading to God, he must go through life again as a human being. Every life is an examination: whoever fails to pass, must try again until he succeeds. That is a Divine law which applies with equal force to all Creation: there is nothing capricious about the ways of God.
"When I tell you that a spirit does not retrograde into a lower stage, the reason is, that although it may have degenerated in one respect it will have advanced in another, so that a balance is struck. Here too you can see the working of a Divine law.

"Of the ages that elapsed from the days of the fall of the spirits to that on which the first fallen spirit was fit to be incarnated in human shape, you can form no conception. "One day is with the Lord as a thousand years, and a thousand years as one day." (2nd Peter 3 : 8.)

"Of all these facts Christendom of today is ignorant, and they run counter to your own previous ideas. But why conceal the truth from you even if you may find it beyond belief and because it may be scoffed at by your fellow men?

You have the opportunity of inquiring into these truths during the spirit-communications at spiritistic services, and if you do so you will find my statements confirmed in every particular.

"Unfortunately the important facts which I have revealed to you have been deleted from the Biblical account of the Creation, until scarcely any of them have been retained. This account says nothing of the creation of spirits by God, nothing of the revolt and secession of the spirits, nothing of the spheres of progress. nothing of the shaping of the odic bodies of the fallen spirits into their various stages, and nothing of the incarnation of those odic bodies into earthly substance. Your Biblical story of the creation of the world describes an original and entirely independent creation, quite unconnected with the creation of the spirits and their fall.

"The original Scriptures contained all of these facts, but when they were revised later, the Powers of Darkness were at work to deprive men of the knowledge of the links in the chain of God's plan of salvation and to withhold from them the consolation of knowing that ultimately everything will return unto God." "This is good and acceptable in the sight of God our Savior; who would have all men to be saved, and come to the knowledge of the truth." (1st Timothy 2: 3.) It was for the very purpose of leading everything back to God, that the material world was created.

"The Powers of Darkness were, of course, much better served by the doctrine of hopelessness and despair, and by the belief in an "eternal Hell" of which your poet has written the dreadful words: "All hope abandon ye who enter here."

"Such sentiments were far more acceptable to the rulers of Hell than was the belief in a merciful God, Who may, indeed, be angered, and punish with just cause, but Who, at last, will forgive His children and call them back to Him. The conception of a Deity has been debased by the doctrine of "eternal damnation" designed only to inspire terror. What is more, that doctrine added to the difficulty of carrying out the plan of salvation conceived by a God Who sent to sinful and suffering humanity this message of all-forgiving affection: "Can a woman forget her infant, forget to pity her babe? Yet even were a mother to forget, never will I forget you." (Isaiah 49: 15.)

"Many passages in your Bible have shared the fate of the paintings by the old masters placed upon the walls of some of your ancient churches. In later times, so-called "church decorators" came and daubed their commonplaces over the masterpieces, so that if today you remove the outer layer of paint care-fully from the walls, the ancient pictures are once more revealed, leaving the beholder enraptured over the great painter's art.
"In the same way the truthful picture presented by the original Bible was defaced in later times. Erring mortals revised the Biblical accounts, omitting what they could not understand or adding their own mistaken explanations. Their successors "improved" further upon the previous work, supplementing and abridging at will. In this way was not only the truth crowded aside, but many things crept into the Scriptures that tend to make a travesty of the word of God. One of your poets coined

the phrase: "Books have their vicissitudes," and unfortunately this is true of the Bible also. Much that it should contain has been eliminated, and much of what it does contain should never have been admitted, because it conflicts with the truth.

"The various "churches" which refuse to acknowledge this fact and persist in regarding your version of the Scriptures as "authentic" are serving the cause of God but poorly. In fact they are doing that cause more harm than good, for even the least intelligent reader of the Bible, and of the account of the Creation in particular, must realize that much of it must be inaccurate, to say the least.

"The falsifications introduced into the Old Testament called forth the protests of God Himself. voiced through the prophet Jeremiah, as witness the passage: "How do ye say. we are wise, and the law of the Lord is with us? But behold, the false pen of the scribes has written falsely. The wise men are put to shame, they are dismayed and taken: lo, they have rejected· the word of the Lord and what manner of wisdom is in them?" (Jeremiah 8 :8,9).

"Elsewhere in the Holy Writ the truth has suffered at the hands of translators who have rendered certain words and phrases of the original text so inadequately as to distort their real meaning beyond recognition.

"From what I have said you can see the reason for the great obscurity and the many misstatements to be found in the story of the Creation as you have it today. Only occasional references retain a faint glimmer of the truth. It is true that some of the stages of the evolution of material creation are indicated, but these are not consistent with facts, in point of number or of sequence.

"The same is true of the Biblical version of the creation of the first human beings, a passage in which the creation of spirits is hopelessly confused with their first incarnation in the human body.

"In the first chapter of the Bible you are told that God brought man into existence as the last act of Creation, after the earth, plants and beasts had already been made. Then follows the statement: "And God created man in his own image, in the image of God created he him; male and female created he them. And God blessed them: and God said unto them, Be fruitful. and multiply ... " (Genesis 1 : 27.)

"It is perfectly true that the two spirits which were the first to be incarnated as human beings and which, as such, bore the names of "Adam" and "Eve", had been formed by God and in

God's image previous to their apostasy. It is also true that He had created them male and female spirits, and had blessed their union. This, however, did not happen after the earth with its plants and animals had been made, but at the time of their creation as spirits. Anything made by God in His image must perforce be a spirit, for God is spirit, and spirit only, and hence, not substance. Therefore, whatever He creates in His image must likewise be purely ethereal. and not partly ethereal and partly material. as is the case with mortals.

"The rest of the Scriptural account of the creation of man contains contradictions even more flagrant, for a few lines further on you are told that God made man out of clay, and, moreover, only the male, at a time when there was no other living thing on earth, whereas, according to what went before, man is said to have been made after all other life had been created. Thus, according to the second statement, God placed man upon a barren earth, and not until then did He create the Garden of Eden into which He "put the man whom He had formed." Still later, it is said that God caused this "Paradise" as you call it, to grow up in trees bearing luscious fruits of all kinds, and that He put the man into the garden to dress it and keep it. Inasmuch as there was no living thing on earth to endanger the garden, it is hard to understand the need for such keeping. Every single sentence contradicts the one which precedes it!

"Compare this picture with the facts as I shall relate them! You now recognize in Paradise that spiritual sphere into which God, after the revolt of the spirits, sent the least guilty of the rebels, partly as a punishment, partly to try them once more. Within this Paradise grew the spiritual tree of the knowledge of good and evil; this was nothing else than God's commandment, which had been given for the purpose of proving the spirits in this sphere and the significance of which they did not grasp. The observance or the violation of this commandment or rather, of this prohibition, would show whether the spirits in the sphere of Paradise were prepared to take sides with God, or whether they had fully determined to join Lucifer. Should they respond to this test by obeying God, the commandment would become for them the tree of life in God's glorious kingdom; should they disobey. it would become a tree of death. They would be driven from Paradise into the realm of Lucifer, and on that day, the day of their spiritual "death", their severance from God would be complete. "For in the day that thou ea test thereof thou shalt surely die." (Genesis 2: 17.)

"Now you will understand why Adam was commanded to keep Paradise, namely, to protect himself and others against succumbing to the temptation to sin by disobeying God. Now you will also understand what the Scriptures mean by saying that after the expulsion from Paradise of the spirits which had shown disloyalty, they were prevented from returning thither by Cherubim "and the flame of a sword." The die had been cast: they had given their allegiance to the Ruler of the Pit. Henceforth the spheres of Darkness were to be their lot; they had no further claim upon the spheres of Paradise, which will remain closed to those fallen spirits until the day on which they are once more admitted to them as a step Heavenward, on their return to God. Then they may reenter the spiritual Garden of Eden, and from it ascend to that glory out of which they were once driven because of their own sins.

"The mocking remark said by the Bible to have been uttered by the Lord on this occasion is also the reverse of the truth. By the Scriptural account, God, at the moment when countless hosts of His children were being driven into the unspeakable woe of utter exile from His kingdom, exclaimed: "Behold, the man is become as one of us, to know good and evil; and now, lest he put forth his hand, and take also of the tree of life, and eat, and live forever, therefore the Lord sent him forth from the Garden of Eden ... " (Genesis 3: 22.) These are the words of a fiend. not those of an infinitely benign God, and as a matter of fact they were spoken by Satan in mockery of the deluded spirits. On the contrary, God wished that even after their fall, those spirits would reach out after the tree of life, in obedience to His will and in an effort to return unto Him.

"But the Powers of the Abyss are intent upon preventing the spirits which were the first to benefit by God's clemency, shown by the creation of the spheres of regeneration, from extending their hands toward the tree of life and from returning to God. Could Lucifer have had his way. those stages would never have been created and no material world would ever have existed. He would then have been able to exercise his despotic sway over those spirits without restraint and without having to fear the loss of a single one of his subjects.

"Furthermore. I must take exception to the way in which the creation of the first woman is described.
"As told in the Script4res, God resolved to give to the first man a helpmate in his isolation. To this end He is said to have formed out of the ground "every beast of the field and every bird of the heavens; and brought them unto the man," in order that he might find a helpmate among them. "But for man, there was not found a helpmate." Then God is said to have caused the man to fall into a deep sleep. during which He "took one of his ribs, and closed up the flesh instead thereof. and the rib, which the Lord God had taken from the man, made He a woman, and brought her unto the man." (Genesis 2: 21, 22.)

"As you know, this story has been made the butt of ridicule. especially among the irreligious. It is a sad thing to see the act of creation so grossly misrepresented and converted into a laughing-matter for mankind. In this instance also, Evil has turned the fair image of truth into a repulsive caricature, through the instrumentality of its human agents and with the view of converting the conception of a sublime and all-knowing Deity into something ludicrous. since to make a thing an object of ridicule is to forge the deadliest weapon for its destruction. God did not prevent this distortion of the truth, as indeed He never intervenes in misdeeds contemplated by man. Seekers after the truth. and the righteous generally. always had means at their command to allow them to discriminate between the true and the false in the altered versions of the Scriptures, being free to communicate with the good spirit world from which they could learn the truth at all times.

"What. then. is the true story of the creation of the first pair of human beings?

"Adam was the first spirit to reach the point at which he could emerge from the higher orders of beasts and be incarnated in the form of man, although his incarnation did not proceed in the manner incorrectly related in the Bible. God did not fashion a human figure out of clay and blow life into its nostrils, thus making man a living soul. On the contrary, the formation of the first man proceeded according to the identical laws which still apply today in the materialization of spirits.

"This is a subject in which I have already instructed you at length, so that you know that nowadays the od of so-called "materialization mediums" is required for converting the spirit-forms into matter.

"This same law was applied by God in the incarnation of the first human spirit. Since, naturally. no human materialization mediums were available to supply the required od, God took the od of the earth. and, incidentally. in a composition which corresponded to that of the human body. The odic mixture was the same as that by which the formation of the human body through growth, takes place today. In the words of Saint Paul: "But God gives to the plant its body as he pleases, to each according to the seed. Neither are the bodies of all living creatures alike. The body of man is unlike that of the four-footed beast, as this again is unlike that of a bird or a fish." (1st Corinthians 15: 38, 39.) The preparation of the od for the incorporation of the first man was undertaken by God's spirit-world.

"The body of the first man whom you call "Adam" was therefore literally taken from the earth, although not in the manner in which you have heretofore believed. No figure was fashioned out of clay. but the ethereal members of that human spirit were covered with a material garment, with the aid of the condensed od of the earth. and that same body of Adam. formed as I have described. was again dissolved into earthly od after his death. It had been taken from the earth in the form of od, and in the form of od it was returned to the earth. That is the law which rules all material creation.

"The first man who thus came into existence was the only one of his kind. As your Bible quite rightly says. he was lonely. surrounded as he was by nothing but plants, and by the beasts of the earth. and longed for the hour when another spirit should have progressed to the point at which it could be incarnated in human form. He therefore looked about among the higher animals to find one which at its death would be considered worthy in God's sight of being advanced to the human stage. Your Scriptural account hints at this when it tells you that God brought all the beasts unto the first man, so that he might choose a helpmate from them.

"The day came at last on which another spirit had reached the human stage. This time it was a female spirit, the same one which had been Adam's consort in God's kingdom and later, in the sphere of Paradise, where it had been the first one to disobey. and in so doing had caused Adam to fall likewise.

"As her guilt had been the greater, so too had been her punishment. Her ascent from the depths had therefore been slower, and she did not reach the level of human existence as soon as did her male dual spirit.

"The story of the incarnation of this female spirit as given in the Bible of today gives a faint inkling of the truth.

"The incarnation of "Eve" as the first woman is called in your Bible took the same course as do all spirit-materialization. In her case it was no longer necessary that God should take the od of the earth, since a materialization-medium, namely Adam, was available. The possession by Adam of unusual mediumistic powers is to be ascribed to the circumstance of the materialization of his own body by the spirit-world. with which he was in constant mediumistic contact.

"Just as today the materialization of a spirit is possible only when the materialization-medium is in a deep trance, so was it in those times. The deep trance into which Adam went is referred to in the Bible by the words: "And the Lord God caused a deep sleep to fall upon the man, and he slept." (Genesis 1 : 21.) This was a mediumistic sleep. in which Adam's spirit left his body. As is the case today, the od of the materialization-medium is not sufficient to effect complete materialization and must be supplemented by substance drawn from the medium's body in dissolved form. so, in materializing Eve, the spirit-world dissolved a part of Adam's physical substance and used it to fashion Eve's body. This proceeding gave rise to the Biblical account of the removal of one of Adam's ribs: "and he slept: and God took one of his ribs, and closed up the flesh instead thereof: and the rib which the Lord God had taken from the man, made he a woman ... " (Genesis 2: 21, 22.)

As a rule, the materialization of spirits lasts for a limited time only, after which dissolution again takes place and the physical substance lent by the medium is returned to him. However, in the case of Eve, permanent materialization was aimed at, and for this reason, none of the od nor the part of the physical substance taken from Adam could be restored to him. Hence the spirit-world had to make his loss good, which it did by drawing upon the od of the earth, as it had done when it first formed Adam's body. This is indicated to you by the Bible in the words: " . . . and he took one of his ribs, and dosed the flesh instead thereof."

"In this way was formed the first pair of human beings, from whom the whole race of man was to descend by reproduction.

"In physical reproduction, the germ alone, out of which the offspring's body is to grow, is transmitted. The spirit is united with that body only moments before birth, in conformity with laws unknown to you. The life of the child within its mother's womb originates with her. It is her blood which circulates through the child's body and sets its organs in motion as soon as they become partially ready to function, which generally happens in the fifth month of pregnancy. This movement of the child's organs while it is still in the womb is necessary, to accustom them by times to the part which they will have to play, and is not, therefore, produced by the child's spirit, which is not embodied until later, but to the mother. It is a process similar to that used in breaking in an engine after it has been finished and assembled: at first it is set in motion by outside power, before being allowed to run under its own. It must be broken in before it is ready for service, and the same thing applies to the bodies of terrestrial living beings.

"God's omnipotence and wisdom are nowhere more evident to thoughtful minds than in connection with the great natural secret of the coming into the world of a new human life, the same thing being true, of course, as regards all other living creatures. In all instances it is fallen spirits which are incorporated in bodies produced by procreation, in conformity with the laws of God conceived with such wisdom that your human understanding could not grasp this Divine secret, even were I to try to explain it.

"Adam and his wife had sons and daughters. (Genesis 5: 4.) The brothers took their sisters as wives, so that when you read in the Bible that Cain, after slaying Abel. fled into another country and "knew" his wife there, this does not mean that he became acquainted with her in the ordinary sense of the word, or that there were in existence people not descended from Adam and Eve. According to the usage of the Hebrew tongue, the word "to know" also connotes having sexual intercourse; hence, as you are told: "and Cain knew his wife; and she conceived, and bore Enoch." (Genesis 4: 17.) The same words are used in speaking of Adam: "and the man knew Eve, his wife; and she conceived and bore Cain." (Genesis 4: 1.)

"Thus all of mankind is descended from the first pair of human beings and constitutes the highest terrestrial stage of progress in the ascent of the fallen spirits. This was the frontier of Lucifer's jurisdiction, and before the Redemption, this was the point beyond which no spirit was allowed to pass. Being lawfully Lucifer's subjects, none could escape from his rule, since he was unwilling to waive his right of sovereignty even in the case of those spirits which had repented of their misdeeds and longed to return to God's kingdom. The surrender of this right had to be forced upon him by a Redeemer, prior to Whose coming all human spirits would be obliged to remain in the human sphere, either as corporeally existent human beings, or as spirits in a sphere of the same level as that of mankind.

"Beyond this lay the great gulf dividing Lucifer's kingdom from that of God. To bridge this gulf. a victory over Lucifer must be achieved. As to how the Redemption was conceived and carried out I shall tell you presently.

"Once Redemption had been accomplished, God contemplated the creation of the spirit-spheres through which the spirits of men could, after their earthly death, ascend to the sphere of Heaven step by step. To create such spheres before the Redemption would have served no purpose, since none of the fallen spirits could have reached them, and through them attained to Heaven.

"In this connection I will call your attention to another matter of great importance, namely, that before the Redemption there lived a great many people who were the incarnation not of fallen spirits, but of spirits from Heaven to whom God had granted permission to be born as human beings. in order that they might help others to attain the true faith in God and thus prepare themselves for redemption. Of these spirits which lived in human form were Enoch, Abraham, Isaac, Jacob, Moses, Joshua, Caleb, most of the prophets, Mary. the Mother of Jesus. and many others whose names do not figure in the original Scriptural documents. After their death on earth. these spirits returned to God's kingdom, since, having taken no part in the secession from God. they had not fallen under Lucifer's jurisdiction.

"As for the spirit-spheres which had been provided for in God's plan of Salvation and through which, by that plan, the souls of men were to ascend to God after the Redemption, these are thirteen in number. I need not describe each in detail. What you, as a mortal, can understand of this subject has already been told to you personally in the many communications imparted through mediums for your enlightenment, by spirits from the several spheres. From their manner of appearance and from their speech you were able to form an idea of their lot in each sphere, as well as of the general appearance of the spheres themselves.

"You have seen those suffering souls which after death went into the lowest of the thirteen spirit spheres, and in them you have learned the meaning of Christ's words: "Cast him out into the outer darkness; there shall be the weeping and the gnashing of the teeth." From them, also, you learned the meaning of those words of the Bible: "The dead know nothing." Those spirits, severed from God and condemned to spiritual death as a result of their unbelief during their life on earth, knew nothing. They were ignorant of their identity as human beings, of their former place of abode, and of the significance of the horrors which they were experiencing in the darkness and which rendered their lot so wretched.

"You could also see that as the spirits rose into higher spheres their consciousness broadened and their attitude toward God became less refractory. You were able, likewise, during these communications to distinguish the different light-effects pertaining to the individual spheres, the colors ranging from the deepest black of the lowest stage, through all hues, to the most radiant white of the uppermost sphere. The thirteenth sphere is of a white too dazzling to be endured by mortal eyes. This is the color that prevails in the sphere inhabited by God's pure spirits, or that which you call "Heaven".

"From what you have seen of the spirits of the lowest spheres you will have gathered how hard it is for them to struggle upward from their lamentable state, since their ascent within those spheres is possible only if they will turn to God. But you yourself have witnessed the rebellious attitude taken by these very spirits toward any thought of God, and in their case it is a great act of clemency on His part to allow them to re-assume human form with the least possible delay, for as human beings it is easier for them, from what they see of God's Creation and learn from their own reflections or from the precepts and example of others, to acquire a belief in God, than it would be in those low spirit-spheres.

"Most human spirits must go back to earth repeatedly, seeing that their lives there again and again leave much to be desired and cause them to fall back instead of fitting them for the higher stages in the Beyond. Consider the lives of most men. Are they not wholly centered on worldly matters? How many ever even think of God? How many firmly believe in Him and live righteously? Ever since the Power of Evil introduced money into the world it has an instrument which gives it an unrestricted dominion over the majority of mankind.

"The time which the spirits of the lower spheres must spend in the Beyond before they are re-incarnated in human form varies in each individual instance. It is determined in part by that spirit's transgressions during its last preceding stay on earth. God is just, and every sin must be atoned for, but He is also charitable, and never punishes His creatures beyond their deserts.

"The spirit-communications from which you learned what you know of those thirteen spheres came through mediums of the most widely varied types. The purpose of this was to convince you of the truth of these communications, for had you received the accounts of all the spirits through one and the same medium, you might have thought that they proceeded from his subconsciousness. As you know, your up-to-date science is always ready to resort to the word "subconsciousness" when asked to explain anything in this field for which it cannot account on purely human grounds, and which it is unwilling to attribute to the working of spirits.

"The creation of the thirteen spirit-spheres was the last act in God's plan of Salvation, and before it could be effected, a far more difficult problem had to be solved. Of what avail were the stages of progress from the deepest infernal spheres to the highest terrestrial-the human-stage, and of what avail were the thirteen spirit-spheres contemplated for the further ascent to the level of God, so long as Lucifer refused to release any of the spirits which had deserted to him, and so long as he insisted upon exercising his sovereignty over them, as a right which God had conceded?

"Who, indeed, could force Satan to waive his rights over those, at least, who longed to return contritely to God? It is true, God Himself could have done so, but from a sense of fairness He had conceded that right to Lucifer, and for the same reason He was now unwilling to withdraw it.

"Only a spirit willing to enter the realm of the Prince of Darkness and to expose itself to the rigors of his tyrannous rule would have the right to do battle with him. The same situation holds good in your international law, when a nation which is oppressed and harassed by its rulers, rises against its tormentors in an effort to shake off their yoke.

But it must be a spirit which would not, by deserting God, become subject to Lucifer, and thus fall irretrievably into his clutches.

It must be a celestial spirit which, after assuming human shape, would invade Satan's dominion in body only, for every incarnated being is exposed to the influence of the Powers of Evil. Hence Evil has so great a hold over all earthly creatures, even over those which are not evilly minded. The most righteous of men daily experience the influence of Evil over them, and often stumble under its impulse.

Thus the undertaking would be a great act of daring on the part of the celestial spirit which would venture upon it. Born, as it was to be, in human form, it would necessarily, as a mortal. remember nothing of its previous existence in Heaven. It would therefore be ignorant of its own identity as well as of the mission for the performance of which it had been incarnated, and would be tempted by the Evil One to sin. Moreover, God would not give it any greater spiritual aid than He gave to others, for this would have offended His sense of justice. It would have to earn whatever special Divine aid might be needed for solving its task, by repelling all advances of evil. and hence would receive such assistance only in the measure in which it withstood such attacks. That is true of all men. On the other hand, as the measure of Divine aid increased, the assaults by the Powers of Evil would grow in violence. God permits temptation commensurate with the power to resist it; children must not be as severely tempted as are adults; shoulders able to bear only half a hundredweight must not be called upon to carry twice that amount.

"By the same token, the celestial spirit that was to assume human form would not be exposed in childhood to the evil influences with which it was to be brought into contact at maturity. Only after it should have discovered its identity and the purpose to be served by its incarnation was Hell to be permitted to unleash its full strength. Then the life and death struggle was to begin, a war to be waged by that spirit as a mortal defensively. Against the attempts on the part of Evil to induce it to abandon God. It must be a war ending in the bodily martyrdom of the incarnated celestial spirit, provided it remained steadfast unto death, since it is the recognized procedure of the Forces of Evil. when their light and intermediate artillery fails to reduce a fortress, to bring up their heaviest batteries in the shape of physical torture, and thus to compel surrender. For this purpose they never lack human instruments and helpers.

"If, in the face of the greatest torments of mind and body which the spirit could suffer as a mortal at the hands of the Powers of Hell and their human agents, it remained faithful and true to the last breath, then indeed it would have earned the final measure of Divine aid and strength which can be granted to any spirit. Armed with this Divine power it could, after its earthly death, enter upon a war of offense against the Powers of Hell, which as a mortal it had been able to meet in defensive combat only. Its victory over Lucifer was then assured, since the warring hosts of Heaven would be at its disposal. "Then indeed there would be a war like that which had raged in Heaven when Michael and his legions overthrew Lucifer with his satellites.

"This time, however, the war was to be fought in Hell, which the celestial redeeming spirit would invade, in order to overcome Lucifer on his own ground. It was not intended to deprive the latter of his sovereignty over the apostate spirits or to condemn him to utter impotence; the victor was to content himself with merely curtailing Lucifer's previous authority, for theretofore he had exercised it not only over those who were with him at heart, but to an equal extent over others who had deserted to him deliberately, it is true, but who now repented of their step and longed to be discharged from Satan's Foreign Legion, in order that they might return to the house of God. By the victory of the celestial spirit, Satan was to be forced to release the penitent spirits from his despotism, retaining the right, however, to employ every means of corruption, as before, in order to bring about another change of heart in them and to bind them to himself anew. But no longer might he keep them under his scepter by force as he had done in the past. He was to be compelled, as it were, to retire his frontier guards from the bridge to be built by the Redeemer, so that no spirit desiring to return to its homeland would be forcibly prevented from so doing.

"Should the Prince of Darkness consent to this limitation of his rights, which, as the vanquished, he was bound to do, and should this limitation be embodied in the terms of the treaty of peace, its observance by Satan would thenceforth be obligatory, since God Himself was to be the omnipotent and just guarantor of that treaty, even Hell being subject to His might and helpless against His arm.

"The consequences of such a peace would in the end be disastrous to Lucifer and his kingdom, for by it, he would lose his subjects one by one, and in the end, be in the position of a captain whose entire forces have deserted to the enemy and who, when at last reduced to utter helplessness, has nothing left but to admit defeat, and surrender.

"In the same way, Lucifer, after having been abandoned by all, would ultimately recognize his impotence before God and be forced to tender his submission.

"This, then, would be the day on which under God's plan of salvation there would be no more separation from Him, no "death". On that day all limbs broken from the tree of life would be re grafted to it, woe and wretchedness would be no more, and all the tears shed in such numbers by His erring children on the long road of their wanderings, would be dried by Him. That was to be the day on which the kingdom of God would once again shine in the full glory which it had before the fall of the spirits, and on which all of His children, who had returned home, would resume the places which once had been theirs in their Father's house.

"Even Lucifer, the last and most penitent of all to cross the bridge built by his Conqueror, would again be the glorious Light Bearer of old, by the side of his brother, Christ, whose love and benign rule he had so contemptuously spurned, and the Heavens would resound with peans of joy.

"Such was the plan of Salvation conceived by God after Lucifer and his angels had fallen, but it was revealed by Him only to His first-created Son and to a few of the holy spirits of Heaven, one of which was to declare itself ready to undertake, when called upon, the dangerous mission of being born of woman, and as a human being, vanquishing the Prince of Darkness. All knew what it meant to assume the human shape. All knew that as human beings they would incur the risk of being overpowered themselves by the very foe they had set out to conquer, and that, in this event, the coveted Salvation could not be accomplished. They knew, too, that a defeat of that spirit sent to earth as a redeemer, would make necessary the sending of a second, perhaps to be followed by others, until the effort was successful. Nevertheless, every one of the high heavenly spirits eagerly volunteered to undertake the venture.

"However, Christ, as the highest of created spirits and as God appointed king over the spirit-world, begged to be the first to be allowed to make the attempt. It was against Him that Lucifer had revolted, and it was on His account that the great secession had come about. It was on His account also that the gulf between the kingdom of God and that of Darkness had opened, and for these reasons He felt that He, and no other, should build the bridge across that gulf to enable all of God's wayward children to make their way home.

"God consented to the incarnation of His Son, to take place when the fallen spirits, in their ascent through the spheres of progress had reached the highest terrestrial stage, that of man, and had thus advanced to some extent, and when, as men, they had given evidence of a desire to return to God.

"The plan was kept secret from all other spirits of God's kingdom as well as from the Powers of Darkness, in order that Hell might have no opportunity of thwarting it. Had the Forces of Evil known the true purpose of the human birth of the Son of God, had they known that His desperate struggle against the assaults of Evil, and His agonizing death were pre-requisite to his victory as a spirit over Lucifer, they would never have tempted Him, and would have done their utmost to prevent, instead of bringing about, His death upon the Cross.

"Only after Christ had died a redeemer's death would the time be ripe to reveal to all Creation God's plan of salvation in its full. inconceivable grandeur, for then its revelation could no longer do harm, but only good. The outer structure of the edifice of salvation being finished, it would be safe against destruction. The completion of the inside work would rather be hastened by proclaiming the plan, for this completion would lie in the fact that the spirits which had forsaken God would now return home over the bridge which the Redeemer had prepared for them.

"Every part of God's plan of salvation that might be revealed to mankind as an anchor for its hopes was to be found in the original Bible, including the truths concerning the creation of the spirits, their revolt, their fall, the creation of the spheres of re-generation as the means for a gradual ascent from the Pit, and the coming of a great, God-sent Envoy as Deliverer. Except for the announcement of the Messiah to come, everything has been expunged from the sacred writings of the Old Testament little by little. Mankind no longer understood these truths, and what men do not understand, they as a rule regard as folly and dismiss from their minds.

"This was true also in the days of Christ. Whatever lay outside of peoples' daily experience or conflicted with the creed inherited from their ancestors, could not be brought home to them then any more than it can today. For this reason Christ did not devote Himself to expounding the foregoing truths at length, but confined His teachings to proclaiming the truth concerning God, the fulfillment of the Divine will, and His own mission on behalf of the Father. Everything else He left to the truth-bearing spirits which He intended to send to visit mankind.

"But even after God's spirit-world had arrived in the role of teachers, only men who had made progress in the knowledge of the truth were able to comprehend the Divine plan of redemption. For the others, it was a diet too hard to digest. There were even many Christians who considered Saint Paul beside himself when he preached on the subject, (2nd Corinthians 5 : 13) and when Paul spoke before King Agrippa in the presence of the governor Festus, about the revelations which he had received, Festus said with a loud voice: "Paul you have lost your wits. Too much study is making you mad." (The Acts 26 :24.)

"You also, when you lay my teachings before your fellow men will be told that they are absurd fancies, and that you have gone out of your mind. It has been the fate of the truth in all ages to be branded as untruth and folly, while at the same time palpably incorrect doctrines as to the Beyond are thoughtlessly accepted as true, are preached broadcast and raised to the rank of religious creeds.

"What I have told you of the Divine plan of salvation you will find confirmed in every detail on a later occasion, when I shall disclose to you Christ's whole doctrine in due sequence as revealed to the faithful. partly by Christ Himself, partly by the truth-bearing spirits speaking through the Apostles and through mediums. Then we will also draw a comparison which will be most instructive to you, between the real teachings of Christ and the Christianity of today.

BIBLIOGRAPHY

Greber, Johannes, 1932 Communication with the Spirit World of God

King James Bible

Greber, Johannes, New Testament

Don Franklin Ministries, 1997-2009 Prophetic Roundtable, Last edition July 3, 2009
www.sonofthesouth.net

Borges, James, from Journal of Borderland Research (Vol, LVI, No. 1, 1st Quarter 2000)

Emoto, Masaru 2010, The Power of Love and Gratitude Made Visible